365 Nights

365 Nights

A Memoir of Intimacy

CHARLA MULLER
with Betsy Thorpe

BERKLEY BOOKS, NEW YORK

THE BERKLEY PUBLISHING GROUP
Published by the Penguin Group
Penguin Group (USA) Inc.
375 Hudson Street, New York, New York 10014, USA
Penguin Group (Canada), 90 Eglinton Avenue East, Suite 700, Toronto, Ontario M4P 2Y3, Canada
(a division of Pearson Penguin Canada Inc.)
Penguin Books Ltd., 80 Strand, London WC2R 0RL, England
Penguin Group Ireland, 25 St. Stephen's Green, Dublin 2, Ireland (a division of Penguin Books Ltd.)
Penguin Group (Australia), 250 Camberwell Road, Camberwell, Victoria 3124, Australia
(a division of Pearson Australia Group Pty. Ltd.)
Penguin Books India Pvt. Ltd., 11 Community Centre, Panchsheel Park, New Delhi—110 017, India
Penguin Group (NZ), 67 Apollo Drive, Rosedale, North Shore 0632, New Zealand
(a division of Pearson New Zealand Ltd.)
Penguin Books (South Africa) (Pty.) Ltd., 24 Sturdee Avenue, Rosebank, Johannesburg 2196, South Africa

Penguin Books Ltd., Registered Offices: 80 Strand, London WC2R 0RL, England

This book is an original publication of The Berkley Publishing Group.

This book describes the real experiences of real people. The author has disguised the identities of some, and in some instances created composite characters, but none of these changes has affected the truthfulness and accuracy of the story.

While the author has made every effort to provide accurate telephone numbers and Internet addresses at the time of publication, neither the publisher nor the author assumes any responsibility for errors, or for changes that occur after publication. Further, publisher does not have any control over and does not assume any responsibility for the website or its content.

Cover design by Rita Frangie.
Text design by Tiffany Estreicher.

PRINTING HISTORY
Berkley trade paperback edition / July 2008

Library of Congress Cataloging-in-Publication Data

Muller, Charla.
365 nights : a memoir of intimacy / Charla Muller with Betsy Thorpe.
p. cm.
ISBN 978-0-425-22257-7
1. Sex in marriage. 2. Married people—Sexual behavior. 3. Married people—Psychology.
4. Communication and sex. 5. Intimacy (Psychology) 6. Muller, Charla—Diaries. I. Thorpe, Betsy. II. Title.

HQ31.M79 2008
306.81092—dc22
[B] 2008010402

PRINTED IN THE UNITED STATES OF AMERICA

10 9 8 7 6 5

May 2009

Acknowledgments

CHARLA MULLER

When a gal from Charlotte, North Carolina, publishes a book, there are lots of folks to thank:

I am thankful to my agent, Sharon Bowers at the Miller Agency, for her guidance and support. To Andie Avila at Berkley Books for her gentle and wise counsel. And to the talented Betsy Thorpe, who bumped into my life at an incredibly auspicious time thanks to our mutual friend, Patti. And to all of the aforementioned for taking a chance on me, of all people!

To my Book Club, a group of bright, passionate women who have been a source of special respite for me over the last fifteen years. To my Tuesday Night Women's Bible Study Group, who taught me that, in Him, all things are possible, even intimacy every day for a year with your spouse. To the fantastic NBGs for two decades of steadfast support, great laughs, and wonderful friendship. And to those special friends and NBGers who shared their intimate experiences, a special thank-you!

I would like to thank my dear friends Carole, Missy, and Kathleen (also my sister-in-law), who walked me in from various and sundry cliffs throughout this process and told me time and time again that, of course, I could write a book–as if it's a perfectly normal thing to do! And to Christy, who still supports me to this day.

To my mother-in-law, who thinks most everything I do is fantastic, even writing a book about her son's sex life.

To my mom and dad, who are a tremendous example of enduring love. I owe them a special note of thanks for entrusting me to write a book that would not embarrass the entire family (How'd I do?). To my brother, one of the most upstanding, compassionate, and superbly funny people I know. To my children, whom I love to the point of ridiculousness. I hope that you are proud of me . . . one day. And to Brad, who embarked not only on a crazy year of intimacy with me, but on the crazy year that followed. Thank you for holding my hand and my heart so carefully these past ten years. You are a great sport and I love you.

BETSY THORPE

I would like to thank Charla for having the courage to tell me her wonderful story over sandwiches, and for believing in me to help her "make it work." Charla, it doesn't get any more fun than working with you! (And thanks to Patti for suggesting I meet Charla when I moved to Charlotte.)

To our agent, Sharon Bowers: Thanks for instantly responding to this project with great feedback, superb ideas, and for finding us our wonderful editor . . . Andie Avila. Andie, you believed in this project from the very beginning, and it's through your enthusiastic stewardship that we are now here in print, sharing Charla and Brad's story with the world. Thanks for all your thoughtful work, and for the time and care you've taken with us.

To my daughters, Georgia and Lucy: Every day with you is a blessing, and I hope one day (much further in the future) you will read this book and it will help you in your own relationships. Thanks to my supportive parents, Elise and Bob, for your willingness to be there for me at any time of the day, and for all the free babysitting. Thanks to my friends in the South Charlotte Literary Babes' Club with terrific advice: Tracey, Tracie, Judy, and Emily, and friends far and wide: Kalie, Rosemary, Sarah, Terri, Tina, Nina, Kris, Nancy, Mark, Kendra, Paula, Jane, Heather, and Jenny. Your friendship through the years has been invaluable. And lastly, to my colleagues at Novello Festival Press, Amy Rogers and Lisa Kline–it's a blast working with you, and thank you for taking on some of my work while I sweated to make this deadline!

CONTENTS

To say yes, you have to sweat and roll up your sleeves
and plunge both hands into life up to the elbows.
–Jean Anouilh

The Offer

When I offered my husband sex every day for a year to celebrate his fortieth birthday, he literally fell over. He was so taken by surprise that he actually stumbled over our son's fire truck, which was lying in the middle of the floor in our den, and landed, with a thud, in his leather chair.

It was a few weeks before Brad's birthday. I was confident and excited about telling him my dazzling idea. Likewise, I couldn't wait for him to accept it.

I extended my hand to help Brad off the chair and led him to the sofa. I hadn't thrown the idea in front of him simply to get a reaction or a laugh. So, sitting side by side, I faced him and repeated the offer to him again–this time more slowly and with more gravitas. "Honey, I'd like to give you sex every day for your fortieth birthday." I closed my eyes, relaxed back into the sofa cushion, and waited. Waited for the shock to wear off and the gloriousness of my offer to sink in. But to my astonishment that didn't happen. Instead, Brad actually *declined* my offer of daily intimacy for a year to celebrate *his* birthday.

"Do you actually mean *you don't wanna have sex* with me *every day* for a year?" I declared in a loud and rather high-pitched voice. I have to admit, I was close to that weird screeching noise that women are prone to emit when they are rendered to a state of utter and complete disbelief.

"That's not exactly true, hon. It's just that I don't want you to *feel* like you have to have sex with me," Brad said.

"I'm your wife. Of course I feel like I have to have sex with you. That's why I married you," I reasoned.

"It's a great idea, I guess . . . I just can't imagine that you really mean it."

I hung in there. "What if I do mean it? What if I really do want to have sex with you every day for a year? I mean, would you really say *no* to such a thing?" I was appalled at the notion!

"Of course not. But are you sure you've thought through this and what it could mean? Why don't you think about this some more and we can talk about it later."

With that, Brad walked down the hall and our conversation ended. I sat on that couch in the family room, surrounded by pictures of us together on our wedding day, and of the kids at Christmas and on our annual summer vacation in the mountains, stunned. That was it? End of conversation? I gave him the ultimate offer–the stuff of fantasy–and he said, "Yeah, not so much." Why wasn't he jumping up and down like a kid in a candy store? Why were there no high fives? No kisses of joy and gratitude, and phrases like, "You're definitely going to win 'Wife of the Year' with this one, honey!"

Instead, he had calmly walked down the hall, and left me alone. This exchange is a great illustration of why I both love my husband and why I'm befuddled by him. I mean, wouldn't most husbands have stripped down to their skivvies instantly, swooning over the delicious idea of fulfilling their sexual desires daily? Wouldn't most men be running down the hall, jerking the covers off the bed, and hopping in, thinking: "The guys at the gym are never gonna believe this"? Well, not the one I married, apparently.

Brad, who is gifted with an uncanny ability to get along with me and a rather inordinately large dose of common sense, wanted me to *think* about it. Well, duh, I *had* been thinking about it, which was why I thought it was such a good idea in the first place! I was a tad bit put off, in fact. Wasn't he interested? Did he think I couldn't stick to such an arrangement?

I didn't feel rejected by Brad, per se. I know my husband well and think he knows my limits better than I, and was aware that this proposal was a mighty big commitment. His initial reticence wasn't a commentary on The Gift and his interest in receiving it, but rather on my ability to deliver it. I could have been offended, yes. But I wasn't–he forced me to think carefully about what I was offering, and the nitty-gritty of how I was going to deliver. Because on some level, there could be cause for concern as I'm a "Big Idea" person, which I used to think was charming but am now realizing can be expensive and often hazardous. I can get caught up in the big picture and ignore the details . . . and then it's too late. Like our annual family photo (a big idea and real memory maker) that no one in my extended family under the age of six really wants to take (small but important detail when you're running around the yard corralling little people). Or our trip to New York City to expose our children to "The City That Never Sleeps." Well, that trip became the trip we'll never pay off. But I still contend that sometimes Big Picture folks bring a lot to the party.

So I made a pretense of thinking about it some more. We didn't talk about it again for a week. But I knew I could and I would deliver the goods. I'm just that kinda gal, or so I thought.

The idea to be intimate with my husband every day for a year had a few origins. The first was that I wanted to give Brad something original for his fortieth birthday. I wanted to give him a gift that no one else, only I, could give him. And intimacy–any at all–certainly fit that bill. All around us people were doing big, expensive, dramatic things to celebrate their fortieth birthdays, including taking fabulous all-inclusive trips with ten of their favorite couples to the Caribbean, running a fortieth birthday marathon, and receiving a Tar Heel blue convertible. I felt like we needed the gift of connection, a gift for our eight-year marriage and ten-year relationship, and not something that would evaporate once a vacation was over, get tarnished, or leave us with indigestion.

There was also something special about this birthday. Hitting forty is significant. That number has long been regarded as "middle age" (think how old our parents seemed when they hit forty), and according to urban myth, it's when men turn to affairs and fast cars, and women to Botox and liposuction. Isn't the forty mark when all kinds of people act out in loony desperation in order to feel young, fit, and attractive? Given that context, maybe having sex every day with your spouse doesn't seem all that loony.

Take away the dread of aging, however, and you get to realize that forty is actually a really cool number. A pregnancy is forty weeks long (although it does seem longer, doesn't it?). Noah cruised on his ark for forty days and forty nights. Mohammed got his first revelation from an angel at age forty. Christ was tempted in the wilderness for forty days. A cleansing bath (a mikvah) in a Jewish temple is filled with forty gallons of water. Spiritually and scientifically, there's a lot going on with forty–not the least of which is that you're halfway to *eighty.*

More people than ever before are hitting that eightieth birthday. Today, if you stay married to the same person, you could be married to your spouse for sixty years. Just a few generations back, people got married early, worked themselves silly, and then died. Now, we have to learn to keep a marriage fresh for sixty freakin' years! New ground, friends. So if you can't survive the seven-year itch and the fifteen-year hives, you might never see a cheesy but sweet golden anniversary party thrown in your honor.

For his fortieth, Brad had made plans to celebrate with a rather elaborate golf trip with his three best college buddies. I didn't begrudge him the trip (the poor guy doesn't demand much), but I wasn't in the position to give him any other material gift. No extravagant watch (he doesn't wear one), no box of über-expensive cigars (doesn't really smoke them), no new car (he already has a not-so-new car that runs fine). Nor did he really want those things (except maybe the car)–he's not really into keeping up with all the latest gadgets, or showing off some bling.

The more I considered the idea of what would make a really special gift for someone's fortieth year on this planet, the more I concluded that, well, I hoped it would be hard to top intimacy with your spouse every day for a year. Those girlfriends who found out later about my gift to Brad were astonished at the length of The Gift–an entire year? Why not a week, or a month? It was as if they wanted to slap me about the head and yell, "What in heaven's name were you thinking?"

Well, here it is: I was thinking big and bold, girls. I wanted to do something so dramatic and different that Brad would *never ever* pause to remember what I gave him for his fortieth birthday. And since it wasn't something tangible, so to speak–a watch on your wrist, a car in your garage, a new driver in your golf bag–then the memory of it had to be pretty significant. I never wanted him to put his hand to his chin in a moment of thoughtful recollection about what on earth had happened for his fortieth birthday. No, I wanted this gift to come crashing down on him in all its awesomeness every time he reflected on it. And I wanted him to smile every time he remembered.

This gift was my personal–very personal–way of showing Brad how really committed I was to our marriage. I had been kicked sideways to the curb by a bout of good old-fashioned depression a couple of years before his fortieth. As depression is so capable of doing, it takes all of your faults and wounds, and wriggles its fingers around to open them up and crushingly reveal them to you. I realized what I was–and more important, was not–made of. And in the landscape of my marriage, I learned that I had married a man so solid, decent, and loving that surely God had a hand in such a lopsided union. Because I'm not sure which is worse–suffering through depression, or watching the person you love struggle with it and take your family life down with it. The ways in which my husband treated me in this state, with such unconditional support and gentle guidance, were awesome. I'm not sure I could have done the same for him in a crisis. In a weird way, I am thankful it was me and not him who had to struggle with depression, because I would be an impatient, frustrated, and smart-alecky spouse, nagging him to just get over it already.

After a year (or two) of being desperately off-kilter, this offer was an acknowledgment that I, too, was committed to the idea of reestablishing a flourishing, happy, and nurturing marriage. And while we had arrived at a comfortable status quo, I had a feeling that our status quo wasn't cutting it. Because of many expected and unexpected tugs and pulls life had thrown our way, intimacy had ended up like that box of Girl Scout cookies in the back of the freezer, hidden behind the frozen pizzas. You know they're still there, but you're not enjoying them as much as you could. Digging them out from under those pork tenderloins can be a hassle.

Let me be clear here–we were never some hyperintimate

couple. The year our daughter was born, I think my husband could count on his fingers and toes (or perhaps just his fingers) the number of times we even had sex at all. I tell you this to iterate just how painfully average we are. It was good when we had it; we just didn't have it all that much. Our sex life took a nosedive very quickly after the honeymoon was over, with the arrival of our daughter thirteen months after our nuptials. It was, not surprisingly, an occasional silent sore point between us, until my husband, bless him, convinced himself for the sake of his sanity that quality was more important than quantity. This was an attitude I was grateful for, but we both knew he was kidding himself. And I was kidding myself that it wasn't important to how I felt as a wife and about our relationship. There was some tension around this, but little time for contemplation as, twenty-three months later, one baby turned into two.

Since our sex life was indeed fairly abysmal as we entered into Brad's fortieth year, I wanted him to know that I was willing and happy to make such a huge about-face for him and for us. I wanted this gift to show him that I valued him and our relationship enough to go do something really nutty like trying to have sex every day for a year. Sex for a week? Certainly doable, probably forgettable. Sex for a month? Well, sure . . . a bit more challenging. But sex for a year? Now that was knock-your-socks-off, the-stuff-that-dreams-are-made-of fantastic. And that was the gift I wanted to deliver.

And the other good news about this life-altering, mood-enhancing, relationship-building opportunity? It didn't cost any money. It wasn't some harebrained idea that required us to take our kids out of school, quit our jobs, move to Alaska, and live in an igloo. We didn't have to take out a second mortgage to finance a trip around the world and take language lessons (*Parlez-vous français?*) before we left. We didn't have to change our lives in order to *change our lives*. We could keep our jobs, raise our family, maintain our friendships, but our whole marriage could change. And it was legal . . .

This crazy idea of mine met all the criteria for a great gift—unexpected, thoughtful, memorable, cost-effective, and especially well suited for the receiver. Did I feel as though I owed this to my husband? Absolutely not. But I wanted him to have it and give the relationship a boost in the way that his steadiness had given me a boost. Despite our differences, Brad (Steady Eddie) and I (Big Idea Girl), for the most part, made a good team. I am a born and raised Southerner; Steady Eddie grew up outside Cleveland. Big Idea Girl attended a giant public university, Steady Eddie a small private liberal arts college. I am loud and irreverent . . . Well, surely you've guessed Steady Eddie is a solid, unassuming guy. And to boot—I really love him.

A week later I approached Brad again—it was a few days before his fortieth birthday. Time was running out if we were going to kick this plan into gear. "I've been thinking about it, and I still want to give you sex every day for a year for your birthday. You game?"

"Of course I am—it's a great gift! I just want you to make sure you feel comfortable with it."

"Of course I'm comfortable with it, it's *my* idea!"

He smiled, relaxing into the idea. "How would it work?"

I was dismayed. "What do you mean, how would it work? Has it been so long since we've had sex that you're suggesting we've forgotten how?"

Brad blushed. "No. What I mean is . . . what are the details, the specifics? Are there some parameters to this arrangement?"

"Well . . . yes, actually. Thank you for mentioning that." This is what I came up with:

We will actually discuss and schedule intimacy. You cannot be married, have a grown-up job, kids to feed, and a house to keep and have passionate, spontaneous connections . . . every day. It is simply not a workable model. You can spontaneously decide to get a manicure on your way home from work or to call your old college roommate who lives in L.A. just to say "hey," but you cannot spontaneously burst into passionate and smoldering lovemaking in the "married with kids" model. And anyone who is married with kids and says they can and they do . . . well, they are lying. This was a hard admission for my guy, who hangs mightily on to the memories of our courtship, back when kids, mortgages, and yard work did not interfere with our ability to burst into a passionate moment at any time.

Brad complained that discussing sex somehow detracted from its loveliness. Fiddlesticks, I said. Since I go to bed early and Brad goes to bed late, timing is important. Nothing is more maddening in my world than entering into a hard-earned hour of REM sleep and having someone nuzzle up to you, getting a feel for opportunities.

Daily scheduling requires some finesse, another adjustment

we had to make. Therefore, television does not trump intimacy. This rule works for two reasons. The first is the undeniable and noble defense that anything on prime-time television (or cable, for that matter) is *not* more important than connecting with my spouse in a meaningful way. The second is that we have DVR, which is a fundamental game changer when it comes to time management of any kind. Now, my husband can pause the football game, I can fold a page in my book, we can have a delicious little romp in the hay, and then return to our lives, already in progress. Quickies count. In fact, quickies often are preferred if you're doing this daily.

Another rule was that either party could decline. I have to say that, being a nice girl from the South, I do not think it is polite for me to offer regrets to the party I planned. So I would decline only under physical or emotional duress. And I just had to think my husband would never, *ever* in a million years (or at least for the next 365 days) decline something that is "so unbelievably awesome" (his words, not mine).

"So those are the ground rules. Whaddya think?" I asked.

"I think that all sounds great. I have some more questions, though."

"Okay, lay it on me," I said. "Oops, no pun intended."

"What about when I'm out of town? Or you're out of town . . . or out of commission, so to speak."

"Hmmmm, yeah. Why don't I get back to you on that," I said.

Just like learning good study habits can prepare you for a

"lifelong love of learning," we needed to work on the basics. And maybe, if we worked on these ground rules, I would acquire a lifelong love of having sex daily. Dare to dream, right?

So, back to the ground rules–when Brad's on the road, there's obviously no sex. And please, phone sex does not appeal to me at all, nor is it in the spirit of The Gift. We are in this for a physical and emotional connection with our spouse, not long-distance pillow talk. In reality, my husband's travel schedule is not that heavy, and we agreed to try to "make up for it," though that is not required, nor will it be tracked and/or counted. No score sheets for us. No play-by-play criticisms.

That leads us to the rather delicate definition of what counts as sex, and what does not (as Bill Clinton was so famously asked). Well, for the purposes of viewing this as a team sport, we did have a rather liberal definition of what counted as a connection, but it did require active participation from both parties (i.e., both parties had to be awake or it didn't count). Regarding other issues (you know, the, ahem, monthly cycle or an occasional UTI) . . . well, we would just try to work around them. Of course, reliable birth control was a must, too. And if I really, *really* had a headache, horrible cold, or some semblance of the plague, then of course no sex. This was not set up to be a marathon or some record-setting contest, mind you, but a considerate and sincere attempt to bond via daily intimacy and connection.

Once we committed to the theory of this arrangement, Brad went back to his *Wall Street Journal*, and I went to unload the dishwasher. There was no big to-do. We did not celebrate in anticipation of The Gift, although I wish we would have had some sort of kick-off celebration. Some champagne would have been nice, as champagne is always nice. Instead, I felt as though we had just moved on to the next task at hand. Birthday present—checked off the list.

While I stood sorting plastic forks and spoons shaped like animals, I was reflective. I simply assumed this would enhance our relationship, but I had to wonder: What if it didn't? What if this was a mistake that ranked up there with my mustache-bleaching incident? What if I couldn't follow through? What if Brad couldn't? What if it didn't do anything to enhance our relationship but simply created stress? What if we grew sick of it and, likewise, sick of each other? What if having more intimacy didn't really make a difference? And while I didn't think this experiment could do any extreme damage, perhaps some nice cuff links would have done the trick.

I mean, on one level I knew Brad wouldn't do anything crazy like leave me—barring something horrendous like infidelity—he had told me as much. But on another, I didn't quite believe it. It wasn't that I didn't believe *him*—I knew his passionate assertion was from the heart. Rather, I was suspect of any rational person's ability to make the claim in the first place. How can any of us know what life will be like ten or twenty or thirty years from now? I was committed to the idea of staying married, but as trite as it sounds, there are simply no guarantees, despite wedding vows to the contrary. In some ways this put me on notice—it nudged me out of marital complacency and into this experience, I guess. But what if I jumped out of the complacency pot into the "Oh no! What in tarnation have I done?" fire? Of course, we'll grow closer, I thought, how could we *not*?

I was getting a little jittery, and it occurred to me more than once, as we approached Brad's birthday, that perhaps these were issues I should have considered earlier. Ah, hindsight.

JULY

Fireworks

"Honey, what if we don't like it?" I asked.

He looked up from the paper, distracted: "Don't like what?"

"Like having sex every day . . ."

He smiled. "I don't know about you, but in my case . . . I think it's pretty close to genetically impossible for me not to like having sex every day." He looked a little more intensely at me, trying to read me: "Are you changing your mind?"

"Absolutely not! I'm just . . ." I hesitated, and then continued, "thinking through some things."

"I don't know, sweetie, it sounds like you're backpedaling. Just say the word, and we go out to a lovely birthday dinner for two and call it a day."

It was an inauspicious start to Brad's birthday. We were on our annual vacation in the mountains at my parents' house.

Dreamy, huh? Wait, it gets better . . . In addition to my parents and my children, my brother, his wife, their toddler, and their new baby were there, too–a family affair, to say the least. *Très romantique, non?* So this was not exactly a secluded, lovey-dovey place to kick off having sex with your husband daily for a year, but hey, a birthday gift is a birthday gift, right? It was a standing tradition that we spend the week of July Fourth up in the glorious mountain town of Asheville. Not even my offer was going to push this trip aside. Perhaps it was sleeping in my old bedroom on July second, the night before Brad's birthday, that made me worry whether I could pull off this endeavor. It had been redecorated since I'd moved out, but my flute was still in the closet, along with my high school yearbooks and my wedding dress, professionally cleaned and packed away for who knows what.

Surrounded by the stuff of old dreams and tossed-aside possessions, I had some lingering doubts as I surveyed the site of what was to be our first attempt at intimacy every day. I mean, if I could throw away my daily commitment to that flute so easily (and I did . . . snap, just like that), couldn't I just as easily dismiss this whole 365-nights-o'-pleasure thing? I didn't want Brad to think that I was reneging on my offer, because I wasn't, but I did want to be honest with him. What if we didn't make it? What if, instead of this being the great year that I had envisioned . . . it turned into the year where Brad chuckled and said, "Char, remember when you made me that great offer and then retired twelve days later?"

Arg.

Brad's suggestion of tossing aside my birthday offer and enjoying a gourmet dinner sounded nice, but it would be only marginally adequate, and we both knew it. I took some nice deep breaths, centered myself, and got back in the Sex Every Day Zone. I could do this. I had promised some serious once-in-a-lifetime action to my husband and I could not be an Indian giver on this one.

This reminded me of a time during our engagement when I was backpedaling for a different reason. Brad was engaged before we met, and I was a little unnerved by that, not because I had concerns about the former fiancée, but rather, what if he changed his mind about getting married, again?

"I won't change my mind," he told me over and over again with extreme patience.

"How do you know?" I asked. "You thought you had it right the first time. What if it's not right this time?"

"Because I know. Because I've been there. Because I know what it feels like to feel right. You should know that there is nothing you can ever do that would ever make me leave you."

"Really? Nothing?"

"Nope."

And that exchange changed the course of our relationship. From then on, I worked harder to make sure that this lovely man who would never, ever leave me had a great life, not in spite of me, but because of me. And while I failed miserably at times, he had faith in me. I had tempted him with this offer of my own making, and he let me know that he wasn't going to let me do it unless I really wanted to. This was all the reassurance

I needed. "Don't be silly. It's going to be great." And with that, I was ready.

There was much to do to prepare, for the actual birthday, I mean. In addition to Brad's birthday, my family gathered to celebrate birthdays for my brother and my daughter. We were surrounded by a dizzying number of birthday dinners, cakes, celebrations, and gifts. There was a whole red, white, and blue color scheme going on, which has always bummed out my baby brother, who swears red cake icing tastes different. He should know as he's had a red, white, and blue birthday cake every year for the last thirty-four years.

Fourth of July parades, cookouts, fireworks, and family birthdays, and you've got a fairly typical July vacation with the Mullers . . . one big, happy family affair. But this year, things felt different for me. Sure, I was nervous about my gift to Brad, but I was also excited. I'd never taken on this kind of commitment before that hadn't fizzled out. Besides employment and marriage, I can't think of anything I've done for an entire year–by choice.

"How in the world will you do it, Char?" I asked myself. There were so many variables to manage–time, energy, availability, nosy kids, ringing phones, housework–the list of distractions was really, truly endless. Even though we had worked out some of the logistics beforehand, the best-laid plans can go amiss. Normally, our mountain vacations included dinner with friends, lots of time at the pool, golf for the guys, some shopping, and serious family time with my parents and brother. Now, we had to incorporate a daily tryst in a bedroom loaded

with tons of nostalgia, including a giant nightshirt from high school tucked in the drawer, ready for wear. It featured a mammoth pink ice cream cone and the words MY DIET STARTS TOMORROW emblazoned on the front. That bedroom did not at all ooze romance, I tell you, including the fact that it was attached to our kids' room via a bath.

But despite my worries, this annual mountain retreat became a giggly, sweet, and fun reintroduction to some revved-up intimacy. The only questions we had to answer were: "Will we do it this morning, this afternoon, or this evening?" I was more relaxed about the chances of our kids interrupting us, because they were so preoccupied with cousins and grandparents and all the play, fun, and games they could ever want, they wouldn't for a moment wonder where we had gotten to. In fact, there was so much chaos and entertainment in that house that no one missed us a bit when we slipped upstairs on our own. I'm happy to report that we did indeed make our kickoff a little flirty and definitely romantic, even while in the mountains with my entire family. Do wonders ever cease?

Some say that it's very easy to be happily married on vacation, but it's much harder to pull it off in the real world. Which is why honeymoons were invented, don't you think? And of course, it's true. On vacation, the stress of everyday life dims in the background of being together. There was no homework to finish, no lunches to pack, no clothes to launder, no meetings to staff, and no conference reports to write. Instead there was golf, massages, long walks, longer dinners, great wine, reading the newspaper, doing a puzzle, and the chance to sleep in (but who can actually sleep in anymore, right?). Even on the drive home from vacation, you can still bask in the glow of a great time together (until your kids get carsick driving down the mountain). But the memories remain. And in our case, the memories of our summer vacation in Asheville remained, too.

However, when our big SUV rolled back into our driveway, the sweet vacation was over. It's amazing how quickly the thrill of vacation is stripped away by forty-three messages in your e-mail box, thirteen more on your voice mail, a spastic cat who is mad that you left and madder that you came home, pounds of mail piled on your counter and sliding onto the floor, some dead plants, and a slightly weird house odor (I know you've had one, too, don't deny it).

It was crunch time–I had to figure out how to live the chaos of everyday life and how to keep my promise to my husband.

So I started at the most logical point–my to-do list. Like everyone juggling marriage, kids, a husband, a semigreat career, a house, church commitments, preschool events, and the occasional girls' night out, my hand cramped before I could even finish writing the list. My to-do list is a work of art, by the way. It is created by hand each week and has three key areas: a day-by-day list; a list of things I need to get done on any one of those days; and a work section that lists all my business commitments. I cross-reference my Kinko's photo calendar with my weekly to-do list to ensure I've not missed anything, and both tools accompany me almost everywhere. As a result, I've got a day-at-a-glance, a week-at-a-glance, and a month-at-a-glance. (I thought about a minute-at-a-glance, but I know when to say when.)

Despite all this preparation for my life, you'd be amazed at how much I still miss and don't get to. And don't pooh-pooh me, and say, well, if you had a BlackBerry or an iPhone or a Palm Pilot, you'd get it all done, and have constant pinging reminders. First, I'm just not that kind of girl. I need a broad visual landscape to see what I have going on, and a tiny little screen with those little thumbing motions just isn't for me. There is something therapeutic in writing it all down. And second, you high-tech planners miss about as much as I do anyway.

Brad's schedule, as the head of marketing for a large manufacturer, is pretty consistent. He leaves early, and unless there is some nutty emergency at work, or a sales dinner, he is home for dinner with me and the kids at 6 P.M. every night. So our opportunities for sex are: morning, before he leaves for work and before the kids wake up; or evening, after the kids fall asleep; and on the weekends, when schedules miraculously mesh and both kids are at a playdate and/or birthday party and we can hunker down in the house . . .*all alone.* Since I am not a morning person, and our kids are up and about getting ready for school, I was pretty much certain that this was going to leave our nightly hours to making whoopee.

This all meant that I had to get organized. Brad and I didn't always agree on how to manage a house–we still don't. But we both agree that neither of us was very good at it at first (and my mother would contend that we still aren't). Negotiating household priorities and chores was hard, as are all things that symbolize power and control. There are a few things he does–occasionally mow, take out the garbage and recyclables, pay the bills, service the cars; and a lot of things I do–cook, make the beds, do the laundry, water the plants; and things on which we tag team–unload the dishwasher, get the kids to bed, tidy up, and so on. Getting to a place where we could manage quiet evenings of "us time"–when the kids weren't waking up crying and the bills weren't getting filed, took a few years of trial and error, but it was a victory that moved us a few steps closer to the giving of The Gift. So when it came to some key logistical issues, we aligned the planets in our favor.

One thing that doesn't make my Kinko's calendar or the weekly to-do list is cleaning. It's just not a huge priority and I'm not that good at it. I am, however, tidy, which is quite different from clean, according to my clean-freak girlfriends. I drive Brad nuts when I sweep the trash, dust, and dead bugs into the corner and prop the broom on top as if to hide it. It will sit there for days and I will add to the sweep pile, until finally Brad scoops pounds of dirt and debris into the dustpan. "You have done ninety percent of the work! I don't understand why you can't close the deal." Ahhh, story of my life, friend. In fact, I loved when my friend moved into an older house in an historic neighborhood and said, "You know what I love best about this house? It has dust in the corners . . . and always will. That's just how old houses are." I couldn't agree more.

But as I said, I am tidy. Like most moms, order comes from necessity because it lends a certain degree of sanity. I wasn't always this way. In fact, I was a slob of great proportions in my single life. I could keep up with my business pretty well despite the clothes piled on the floor, the unopened mail (Bills? I have bills?), the mildewing laundry, and the three inches of dust on my lampshades (and I thought that lamp had a dimmer!). There was even this embarrassing story my senior year where I think I managed to change my sheets just once the *entire* semester. Totally gross, I know now, but on that military-style top bunk, it was really hard to tell they weren't in tip-top shape. My mother came on parents' weekend and was so horrified she had them washed and back in place before Senior Brunch the next day.

But no more. Because I work two days a week from 9 to 5 at the office, and conference call, check e-mail, and return calls on the days I'm not, I'm pretty connected to work. I also have two different sitters: my mother-in-law comes on Tuesdays, and another longtime sitter comes on Wednesdays. For them and for me, it's important to have a fair amount of order so that the mile-long to-do list can be tracked and executed. And because my kids have told me time and time again that they don't like my "mean Mommy" voice, I have decided that I need to do all that I can to make mornings run smoother (and afternoons and evenings, for that matter). Everyone is a shade or two happier, and then I can use my artificially sweet Carol Brady Mommy voice. For me, that means a neat kitchen, school clothes laid out, backpacks stored in a locker, and a reasonable amount of clean laundry piled on my bedroom floor for me to pick through as needed.

When it comes to kids, I am pretty vigilant about bedtime. Since my seven-year-old daughter starts school at an unseemly hour (7:30 A.M.) and since we have to get up at about 6:30 A.M., my kids are fed, bathed, and in bed by 7:30 each night (give or take thirty minutes). Girlfriends have been known to call me at 7:42–"I know that I am calling you at the worst possible time, but . . ." Well, no actually, I think, as I sit back, put up my feet, and sink into my down-filled sofa. My kids are in bed, possibly even asleep, and all is good with the world.

So while the day is a hurricane of drama, tears, pressure, activities, chores, phone calls, carpooling, e-mails, and the chronic challenge of putting an edible dinner on the table, the evenings are fairly manageable–*after* 7:42 P.M. And while I hustle to get things organized at night, I do have a witching hour. If it's not cleaned up, put away, or stuck in a cubby (or somewhere close enough) by 8 P.M. (okay, 7:42), it's not going to get cleaned up and stuck in a cubby or somewhere close enough. You'll find me in a corner of my couch, trying to regain my sanity in front of a mind-numbing episode of *Entertainment Tonight*. Yes, I could be planning my takeover of the world, or darning socks (really, my mother once asked me to locate my basket of clothes that needed darning . . . can you stand it?), taking a painting class, trying out new recipes, but I need downtime, and by that I mean putting things *down* and then putting my hand on the remote.

This is unusual, I know. My girlfriends who work full-time are just sitting down to a family dinner at 7:30, and my girlfriends with commuting husbands claim any bedtime before 9 P.M. means no one sees Daddy at all. But for now, my kids need ten to twelve hours of sleep, so they don't have early-evening activities, and Brad has a job and a commute that gets him home by 6 for a family dinner. My life is hardly picture-perfect, but on this front, I have no complaints. And I have to say that except for the occasional episode when my daughter is convinced she's going to vomit from some unknown bugaboo, and after all the wailing and drama, she just belches loudly and rolls over and goes to sleep, it works out pretty well.

In the old days, before these daily encounters kicked off, I would hop on the computer, plug into a few mindless hours of television, or read a book. Brad would do the same–we have multiple TVs, two computers, and a lot of books. Sometimes we were together watching TV or reading, and sometimes we were doing our own thing. When we weren't having sex regularly, Brad was always wondering if he was going to have sex anytime this month, and I was guiltily wondering when I was going to have the time, energy, or desire to have sex anytime this month. Sex permeates a relationship *more* when you're not having it. Even snuggling on the couch was sometimes fraught with tension–is this foreplay or simply hanging out? Does he expect this fantastic smooching to be something more than fantastic smooching?

While I was very nervous about how this yearlong project was going to fit into our lives, I discovered we did, indeed, have time for intimacy, and that this everyday business really takes the tension out of nonsexual encounters. I can still get my downtime and Brad can have his downtime, and then we can meet up and have some saucy times together in the bedroom.

Once I acknowledged that I used to try to get out of sex, and once I saw how much happier Brad was as a result of our daily arrangement, I asked him his thoughts about my Dance of the Darting Spouse. Brad shocked me with his simple response.

"Well, hon . . . It really sucks to get rejected all the time."

"I don't understand . . . It's not like you should take it personally." I cringed.

"Why not? I'm your husband. How do you want me to take it?" he replied sharply.

Well, that's a veddy, veddy good question.

My intention was not to reject *him*, per se, but rather his request for intimacy. It never occurred to me that he treated those two points as one in the same. But when I said no to his overture, it was a personal rebuff for Brad, and I venture he's not the only guy who's felt the sting of rejection, especially when it piles up day after day like unclaimed coat-check tickets. I felt crummy. Brad's not a complainer, and while there was tension between us pre–The Gift, it wasn't like we were fighting constantly about our lack of intimacy. He wasn't standing up yelling about his rights as a husband, or demanding that I acknowledge his feelings about the subject. I had made out Brad to be this tall, silent, macho type whose feelings couldn't be hurt . . . and shouldn't be hurt when it comes to sex. I had wrongly assumed that he could shrug off my "not tonight" and immediately intuit that I was worn out, stressed, and simply not in the mood.

I sucked at seeing through that facade, I admit it.

While I felt awful that I couldn't change the way I'd behaved in the past, I could do something about the here and now. I've made a big turnaround. Now, I'm doin' it with my spouse . . . yes, the Dance of the Daily Deed.

In that first month, I took a mental note of how it was going: Pure and simple, my husband loved it, as you would expect. He was just so darned happy that he was very nearly beaming all the time. Me? Well, I was beaming, too . . . What's not to love about your husband acquiring a new little shake in his walk and knowing you had a little something to do with it? Prior to July 3, 2006, there had never been a day (or night, or weekend, for that matter) when I'd had sex with my husband and later considered it a waste of time. On the contrary, when we did and do have sex, I usually say, "Wow, that was really nice. We should do it more often." Which slays Brad, it really does. And now that it's every day, I still feel that way, only I don't need the "more often" part.

I've definitely noticed how much more attuned we are. I know it sounds corny, but it's true. My husband feels more connected to me because we're getting to it daily, and I feel more connected to my husband because he, well, he's truly digging me right now. And how great is that? Now please know that my husband is a great guy, great father, and great husband, and I didn't enter into this agreement to correct any sort of aberrant behavior in him. Brad is as steady as they come, and doesn't act out, or whine and complain (unless it's a football weekend and his beloved Buckeyes are losing). He fulfills all his roles–dad, husband, employee, son, brother–with aplomb, and not even a knock on the head could set him off his path. My husband is still his great self, but now he's plussed up.

I benefited from his newly energized self almost immediately. The weekend was coming up, and so I asked Brad:

"Hey, honey, what's on tap for you this weekend?"

"Well, I thought we could have some great family time together on Saturday morning, then I could work in the yard in the afternoon, then we could take a nap and have a roll and then I'd love to take you to dinner. You know, I really like that book you gave me on the boxer from South Africa. Maybe we can talk about that tonight at dinner. Isn't he one of your favorite authors? And while we're at it, how about Italian tonight?"

I was speechless. Before The Gift, Brad would have happily gone along with whatever I had planned for the weekend (except for the yard work part) and was quite content to let me plan evenings, confirm the sitter, and make the reservations. And while we generally had a good time together, I'm usually the Julie McCoy, cruise director of our family, looking out for the next fun thing to do, and he happily tags along for the ride. Now all of a sudden he was really plugged into me, and looking at our calendars, and initiating activities. It was like we were dating again . . . ahhh, remember those days, girls, when it was all about *us*?

I realized an unintended beauty of my gift was its unconditionality. My gift was sex every day, no strings attached . . . no need to catch a feel in the bathroom when we're running late for soccer practice, or to wine and dine me at overpriced restaurants, or to even compliment how my shoes and handbag match (they never do). Essentially all the corny things one unenlightened husband might do to guarantee and/or enhance the delivery of sex, well, they didn't matter. I was going to have sex with my husband every day (barring any of the considerations outlined earlier) no matter what. Sure, if he had acted like a complete jerk and had been incredibly rude and offensive, it might have changed things, but it's not in his makeup and therefore not a likely consideration.

But here's the incredible part: There was absolutely no reason for my husband to do things like attentively listen to me drone on and on about my friend's husband's crazy sister, or help me fold laundry (I'm not kidding), or offer to stop by the grocery store on the way home from work, or schedule a surprise massage for me, or take the lead on planning our family vacation . . . *aside from him genuinely wanting to do those things.*

And I loved that he wanted this. One afternoon, I looked at Brad with all the joyful giddiness of a girl on a date with the man of her dreams, trying to act casual, but really feeling a little breathless about this great fellow sitting next to her.

"Honey?"

"Hmmmm?" he called out from behind the paper.

"I love you."

"I love you, too, sweetie."

"No really, I love you and I thank God every day that we're married. There is no one else on earth I would rather be married to."

"Wow, that's a really nice thing to say. Thank you, honey."

"You're welcome. Wanna head to the bedroom?"

"Sure, but we've done it today."

"I know."

I was basking in the glow of Brad's newfound attention. But in the back of my mind lurked a cautionary tale. "*Remember the wings!*"

it whispered. As with most cautionary tales, it came from those hazy, crazy young adult days. When I was first living in New York City with my friends from college, we lived on the Upper East Side. My roommate and I lived on the first floor of a five-story walk-up.

To my mind, the best time to live in Manhattan is after college and before you have acquired any actual standard of living. Going from sharing one bedroom with three other girls in college to sharing a 1,200-square-foot (which is mansionlike), one-bedroom apartment was actually a step up. While our teeny living area held only a love seat, a wicker chair, and a television, and our hallway was jammed with a chest of drawers we found at the curb, it seemed larger than the house we shared with thirty-two other women. And the bathroom-to-girl ratio was better (*and* you didn't have the "throw-up" toilet to contend with . . . you all know what I mean).

Two other friends from college conveniently lived on the third floor of the same walk-up. It was like college living, but in the big, bad city. New York was kind to us newbies, though, and we all had landed good jobs that allowed us to cover our outrageous rent. We even had enough left over for dollar drafts at a dozen bars on the Upper West Side. And we could all chip in for our Wednesday night ritual: our embarrassing TV addiction (back in the day of *90210* and *Melrose Place*), a few dozen Atomic Wings, and a pint of Ben & Jerry's New York Super Fudge Chunk Ice Cream. In those days, you could *never* have too many wings, too much ice cream, or too much Heather Locklear.

But one night something went terribly wrong. Was it bad chicken? The stomach flu? I'll never be sure, but all those wings and ice cream no longer agreed with me. After the girls went home, I spewed like a fire hydrant. I have never barfed that violently, *ever* . . . not even when I ran into my aunt's house in the country after playing in the sun and unknowingly chugged from a pint of buttermilk. I have never known an hour that dark and vomitous. I really thought I might die or at least barf up some pretty important internal organs.

It was in the dead of winter and our radiator was pumping hot acrid heat into our little bedroom. I needed some arctic air. So I crawled to the den, opened up the window, and pressed my clammy face against the bars on the window, inhaling giant gulps of noxious city air, and then cried like a baby. I was homesick, wretched and wretching, and really wanted my mommy there to soothe my sweaty brow and rub my tummy.

No wing of any kind has crossed my lips since. And while I do still enjoy Ben & Jerry's, it's now Low Fat Brownie Yogurt. The more important issue is that I learned a valuable lesson . . . too much of a good thing–a superrich, fabulously indulgent thing–is bad.

I wondered if the principle applied to sex as well.

I had no one to go to for advice on what the future held for us. I didn't know if we would hit a wall, like marathon runners do in the middle of the race, or whether we would reach a plateau, like dieters do. There are no sex-every-day gurus out there. At least as far as I know. Friends I could turn to? Well, if there were a lot of married people out there having sex every day, it's certainly not dinner-party chatter in my 'hood. And it's not like I could consult my mother–I love her dearly, but she's not that kind of open, flower-child mom who is breathlessly waiting for me to ask her about her life "with" my dad. That would be enough to make her choke on her chardonnay. Women's magazines, another potential source for information, report that married people are having *way* more sex than single people anyway, but beyond that it's all about twenty ways to have your best orgasm ever. (Numbers on a magazine's cover are very important, have you noticed?)

I can't be sure that I read it in a magazine, but I remember once reading that it takes twenty-eight days of doing something to get into a habit. Is that true? I wondered. If so, what kind of habit? I mean, taking a vitamin every day requires you only to remember to take it, and boom, you're done. Leave the bottle on the counter at night and it's a visual reminder. Now this could hold true for sex. Brad is certainly a visual reminder that I should have sex with him every day. I could just picture him walking around with a sign slapped across this forehead: TAKE ME DAILY FOR INCREASED HAPPINESS. ABSOLUTELY NO MARITAL SIDE EFFECTS! Could this catch on as a habit that I do every day, like brushing my teeth and taking a shower? But geez, having sex every day–surely it's a different equation? It seems like time-consuming habits (i.e., something that takes more than two minutes)–like sex, exercise, blowing out your new haircut as well as your fabulous hairdresser does, or anything that requires significant time and concentration (which a good blow dry does, by the way) can be really hard to integrate into your daily routine.

I don't know if anyone noticed a change in me . . . or noticed that I was no longer a standard fixture at every girls' night out. But *I* noticed something. Brad and I flowed better as a couple. We were happier (yes, I was happier having sex every day, but it was only July). Our house ran better because we were both more agreeable, more helpful, more solicitous to each other. And our time together was truly about us, not the promise of special date-night sex. I told my best friend about the arrangement. Not because she was interested in the sordid details of my sex life but because we share with our best friends the stuff that's going on in our lives, especially the good stuff or the surprising stuff or the stuff you never counted on. Like the fact that I was really digging this daily intimacy thing.

I told my best friend that, for sure, I was going to keep going . . . at least through August.

AUGUST

Bikini Daze

"Hon, this sex every day thing would appeal to every husband in America, right?"

"I don't know . . . I guess it would depend . . ."

"On what?" I asked.

"On whether you liked your spouse, and were attracted to her enough to want to have sex with her every day,"

"You mean, if you're married and you weren't attracted to your spouse, you couldn't have tons of sex with her?"

"Absolutely not. I couldn't have done this if I wasn't attracted to you."

Well, *that* was nice to hear. I just assumed that if you're married and you're a guy, you're happy to have sex any way you slice it. And if that slice is sweet, skinny, and cute, great. And if it isn't, so what, you're still getting some lovin'. Brad was surprised at my surprise. In fact, he was a little disappointed that I didn't think more of him and his gender. He claims that to do it every day requires a certain amount of attraction–physical and emotional–to your spouse. So score one for this girl in her thirty-ninth year–I am still attractive to my husband! Apparently this is better news than even I thought–because the reality is that, on average, after three years of being "together," attraction can wane between couples, especially sexual attraction. We've been together for a decade and we're throwing off the curve–good news.

Attraction is an interesting topic to me, because I've never known what it feels like to be the prettiest girl in the room. (Brad disagrees; isn't that the best?) I've come to be okay with that. And while my husband is never going to be on the cover as *People*'s Sexiest Man Alive, he's a great guy, despite the stuff that makes us human. Like when he first wakes up in the morning rubbing his belly and breathing dragon breath; but hey, morning is not my best time either. Every couple has a laundry list of spousal irritants that run the gamut from snoring to losing the remote to making snarky comments about one's mother-in-law (none of those apply to us, of course). I remember a friend once telling me that on some days she wakes up and looks at her husband and thinks, "Mmmm, I could just eat him with a spoon." And on other days she wakes up and looks at this same man and recoils in horror, wondering, "What on earth was I thinking?" And then she remembers that he probably does the same thing.

And I guess that is the chronic balancing act of marriage–some days are great and some days just aren't–but here we are.

Attraction is not just about physical appearance; it's about an amalgamation of things, really. Depending on the occasion, I can be witty, fun, decently dressed, and a really good friend; now that I've decided to make it a priority, I'm also a pretty sexy wife! And while there are a million ways to look, feel, and act sexy–for me, sexy is feeling confident. Clichéd, but true. And since my little project has taken off so nicely and Brad and I are genuinely making time for each other, what's not to love?

These days, a pretty standard routine to feeling sexy takes place once the sitter has arrived, usually at 6. I take a glass of wine to the bedroom, turn on some music, and spend forty-five minutes showering and getting ready. I put on perfume (which is rare), I wear mascara (also rare), and I iron my clothes (very, very rare). Why does this feel sexy? Because now that I'm a mom, I rarely have forty-five minutes to spend on myself during the day. A mom's day is full of making sure her kids look presentable, but there's precious little time to make herself presentable. It's pure pleasure to take the time to make myself look pretty, uninterrupted. After all, getting pretty can lead to feeling pretty and then I walk into the den and Brad stands up and says, "Wow, you look great! Let's go." He takes my hand and we kiss our precious children good-bye and we go. Alone, or with others, it doesn't matter. We're out, I am made up and freshly pressed, I am with my husband, and I'm feeling a little sexy . . . a walking cliché.

Thinking of all the variables when it comes to long-term

couples wanting sex, desiring sex, and ultimately getting sex, I was kind of stumped. What comes first–sex or sexy? It's just one more tired spin on the chicken-and-egg theory–does having sex make you feel sexy or does feeling sexy make you want to have sex? Since we had a time line on this daily arrangement, I didn't really have the chance to probe this conundrum, because we just jumped right into daily intimacy.

I didn't run out and have a makeover before Brad's birthday. There were no coy little games, no cloying love notes. No flowers. No special lingerie. Just the basics. I guess I didn't feel particularly sexy when we started our daily dalliances. Nor did I feel unsexy. And it was okay. There was a practicality to this gift that was difficult to get around–*and* the fact that Brad and I had been together a decade. But once we got in a groove and I realized how much Brad was really, *really* enjoying this gift, I did feel good, better, and yes, even sexy.

To be honest, my moments of feeling sexy and pretty were restricted to home and when I was going out with Brad. Sadly and rarely were these feelings transferring to my time at the swimming pool this summer. Insecure is what I feel at the pool, surrounded by half-naked people, most of whom look better than I do in a swimsuit. But from the relatively safe viewpoint on my lounge chair, beneath my broad-brimmed hat and knock-off sunglasses, I realize that the pool is a giant fishbowl of attitudes about what it is to be a woman stripped down. We apply vats of sunscreen to our bodies, avoiding premature aging, and the kids run and scream and jump in the water. The children wonder why the pool is always empty during "adult swim"; meanwhile on the lounge chairs there is assessing, gossiping, admiring, wishing, showboating, or skulking in and out of the water.

I wonder as I look around–who is getting some good loving? Is it the knockout women or the regular moms–like me? All shapes and sizes are represented here–women in bikinis with killer abs and gorgeous legs (some of whom I still allow to be my friends) and women in skirted tankinis and T-shirts (some of whom are also my friends). Looks can be deceiving, can't they? Because the truth is we don't know who has a dynamite sex life and who doesn't. It's hard to hide cellulite and a baby belly at the pool, but it's quite possible to camouflage a floundering sex life. People do it every day, regardless of what they're wearing. And I'm not sure on whom to place my bets because, sixty days ago, I would have never bet on Brad and me to be a benchmark for an active sex life.

The pool landscape looked so different when I was a kid. Back then, you arrived at the pool at 10 A.M. sharp and stayed until dinnertime. I used to enjoy a Grape NeHi and Nabs while sitting on a tall brick wall watching teenagers play Ping-Pong. The Little Board and the High Dive Board loomed over the pool, and it was the ultimate rite of passage to graduate to the ten-foot-high board. The pool was in its heyday.

I vividly remember a neighbor who was always at the pool and whose dad had run over him with a riding mower (by accident, of course). He had an artificial leg below the knee, but he was freakishly athletic. At the pool, he looked like a bird sailing off that High Dive. Half gainers, two-and-a-half flips. It was beautiful to watch and probably dangerous to do. Today, there are no teenagers at the pool unless they're working there. If I had to pinpoint the demographic shift at the pool, it would have to be with the decline of the High Dive. Today, pools are nice and sterile and safe–to the point of boredom. No High Dive, no diving in the shallow end, no foosball, no unsupervised activities. Just kids and toddlers coated in sunscreen, and parents who trail after them.

Back in the day, my mom would line up her chaise with her girlfriends, pull out her oil, and proceed to smoke, gossip, play an occasional hand of cards, and sunbathe until dusk.

She paid just enough attention to my brother and me to ensure we didn't drown, which we didn't. She rarely played with us in the pool. Playing in the pool with your kids was counter to the concept of the pool back then. You brought your kids to the pool to play with *other people*, not you. She occasionally came in the water, but only to cool off and she never, ever got her hair wet. None of the moms did–it could really mess up those stylish dos from the swinging seventies. I do remember she wore a bikini the color of an orange Creamsicle, which popped nicely against her tanned, caramel-colored skin.

When I was growing up, I thought my mom was *gorgeous*. She personified for me what it was like to be an attractive woman. And when she signed up to be a room mother at school, I thought I would nearly die from pride when she came to my classroom. I grew up in a town with an unusually large Greek population (and great diners), and every school year you were bound to have a Zourzoukis, Tsiros, or Apostolopoulous in your class. Which meant that you would have the most awesome Greek pastries at all classroom events because those mothers also signed up to be room moms. But what my mom couldn't do in the kitchen (which wasn't that much, really) as a room mom she made up for in style. There was always some Greek mother handing out souvlaki that would melt in your mouth, but it was my mom in some hip poly-blend pantsuit, wildly fab hair, and giant sunglasses who stole the show (at least in my memory).

To make things even more fantastic, she smelled great. This was because of her signature scent, available only at your local drugstore–"Charlie." She thought it was so campy that she wore a scent with the same name as my dad that she did it for far too many years. I remember wondering if I would be lucky enough to marry a man named after a perfume fragrance (Calvin? Halston? Ralph?). My mother spritzed Charlie on her wrist and neck every Friday and Saturday night before she and her Charlie sashayed out the door. I remember lying on her powder blue sateen bedspread watching *Hee Haw* and *The Lawrence Welk Show*, while she sat at her bureau and primped. Lipstick, earrings, lots of hairspray, and Charlie (both of them)–let the evening begin. Perhaps our primping rituals are something we inherit from our mothers–proof that taking time to feel pretty and sexy is, on occasion, a worthy endeavor.

Mom would be horrified to know that nobody is kicking back at the neighborhood pool anymore. Life, like the pool, takes work. Before leaving to go to the pool, I can't just throw on a suit and some sandals and go. Well, I guess I could, but I won't for pride's sake, as I'm knocking on forty's door. I have to shave and pluck, put on some lip gloss and moisturize. I have to find towels, goggles, snacks, and a beach bag. I have to track down spare change for the vending machine and snack bar, and make sure I grab my cell phone, too. Once there, I have to position myself so I can keep a keen eye on my kids and make sure they don't drown. No, the moms at the pool aren't smoking, drinking, or playing cards, although those aren't bad ideas. Instead we're coating ourselves in designer sunscreen, drinking bottled water, and making sure our kids haven't lost their eighth pair of goggles of the season.

And there is nothing less relaxing than if you get conned into helping out with the kids' swim team. It was a hell like I have never known. It must have been payback for something I did to someone–I don't know what and I don't know whom. But I was being punished for some unpardonable sin. There could be no other reason why I was put in charge of the bullpen at my children's first swim meet of the very first season of our family's very short-lived swim team career.

For those of you unfamiliar with the swim team bullpen, as I was until five minutes before I was thrust into the flaming throes of this inferno, it's an area where you assemble, coordinate, and line up, *ohhhhh,* say, *185* swimmers before each heat. There were hundreds of kids, and I was supposed to corral them into the appropriate lane at the appropriate time to swim the appropriate heat. There were approximately fifty races over a three-hour period. Perdition, my friends, there is no other word for it.

And to think that just minutes before I had walked into the meet with a chair, my sunglasses, and a chilled bottle of Fiji Water, ready to relax and watch my talented offspring compete. Instead, I watched my seasoned swim meet friends sit in chairs, relax, and watch *their* children compete and look knowingly my way, tsk-tsking with sympathy. Poor Charla, she got the bullpen her first time out.

But what doesn't kill you (or cause you to kill others) does make you stronger. Being responsible for the bullpen made me realize some important things. For example, daily intimacy is way easier–and much less stressful–than working the bullpen at a swim meet. This is valuable on the occasional day when I could take or leave sex–days when either work or a long time outside in the heat by the pool causes me to crave sleep over sex. Then I can remind myself that at least I'm not working the bullpen.

I also learned I have severe personal space issues. The mob mentality of seven- and eight-year-old kids as they form a tight circle around you, pressing, pressing, pressing in on you to determine if they're swimming in the butterfly relay and then asking you again, again, and again . . . and yet again if it was lane 4 or 5 . . . well, it's cause for hyperventilation, I tell you. And all kids look alike when they have on a swim cap, goggles, and matching swimsuits. Telling them apart is like telling apart seagulls at the beach–you can't. You can only stay out of their way as they descend on you for food and hope that the poop doesn't land on you. And I learned that my keen sense of humor and sardonic optimism have strict time limits. After approximately two hours–poof!–they are gone and I become cranky and surly. And I am not remotely placated when the "mom in charge" flies by and gives me a squeeze, a smile, and tells me, "You're doing a *fantastic* job." Which is also further testament to the fact that I did *not* miss my calling to be a second-grade teacher. Not that I ever felt a calling to be a second-grade teacher, but I can now retire for good any thoughts of the sort.

That afternoon I left the swimming pool sweaty, frazzled, and stressed out. Not the vision of my mother at the pool–relaxed, rested, and blissed out. In fact, I later saw photos from the swim meet and I was squinting at this vaguely familiar figure in the background of one . . . Wow, who is that poor woman, I thought. It couldn't possibly be me, now could it? But it was, it was sadly, really me and let me tell you that working the bullpen at a swim meet does not make for an attractive look.

What is it that turned the pool from a place of pleasure and respite into such a spectator sport (and I don't mean a swim meet). Fun, boredom, vanity perhaps? Men do it, too, but women have made an art of it. There is not a more vulnerable part of the poolside day–at least for me–than when my kids whine, "When are you getting in the pool, Mommy? Please get in the pool." Then I sigh, slip off my cover-up, and plow into the water. At this point, it's good to remind myself that while I'm self-conscious in the water with my kids, my husband is attracted to me. Still.

I'm a bit of a realist about some things (not all, mind you, but some), including body image: You see, I'm a sturdy girl. There, I said it. I know it's true, so don't think I'm fishing for you to tell me I'm not. And I know it's not a good thing. And I could be healthier and I could exercise more, and blah, blah, blah. Weight has been an issue for me since . . . well, let's just say for a long time. I remember walking down a street in Manhattan in my twenties and passing two women discussing bathing suits, and which kind looked good on them. And one said to the other, "Honey, my bikini days are *over*!" And I thought to myself, "Me too, hon, me too."

In fact, I haven't worn a bikini since the age of five. That was the one summer when my mother dressed us both in matching leopard-print bikinis (she does have fantastic style, remember). After that, I took control of my wardrobe and I knew that leopard-print bikini was my last. It remains a fond memory for my mother, though, perhaps because it was the last time she, too, wore a bikini. Just to test the bikini waters for the last time, I did purchase a bikini in high school–it had a little flouncy bottom and a floral top. I didn't look bad in it, I just didn't look *good* in it. Therefore, it never saw the light of day, or knew the smell of chlorine. I resolved that the one-piece suit was where it was at for me. So it was, so it shall be forever more.

Post-kids, body image gets even worse. Few women can pull off a bikini after pregnancy–our bodies have betrayed us in ways we never thought possible. This they should teach in sex ed class, and the teenagers with the super-fit physiques would run screaming for the woods. I'm talking wrecked belly buttons.

Squishy bellies. Stretch marks. And boobs? Ugh, don't get me started. Sure, there are those who defy the laws of nature and manage to have a taut belly after baby number three, or have boobs that are still perky, and of them I am in awe. I want to *know* their secret. Good genetics? Great personal trainer? Flawless plastic surgeon? Good genes is the one that gets me, because that is just plain unfair. It's like they're getting it for free. Discipline and money? Well, that doesn't seem so bad, because at least they're working for it somehow.

As much as I'd like to think we outgrow this insecurity, not to mention curiosity and competition among ourselves, we don't. My mom, who still looks great in her early sixties, and is living a dream as a snowbird in Florida, aspires to look good during her water aerobics class. And I can assure you, she's got tabs on who's got the goods in the bathing suit department.

I know that men aren't immune to this either; Brad has some body hang-ups, too. He's in fairly decent shape but contends he still spends his pool time sucking in his gut, and wants to scream when a good-looking woman can't take her eyes off his man boobs. "Hey? My eyes are up here!" he's shared with me, only halfway kidding (I think). But he's a sport and he's always splashing in the pool and swimming with the kids–man boobs and all.

Everybody, it seems, has body issues. One girlfriend with curly hair wants straight hair. Girls with curves want to be skinny, and skinny girls want bigger boobs. Hair, lips, eyes, ears, nose, body–we hold ourselves up to that mirror, mirror on the wall waiting to hear that we're the loveliest of all, but every affirmation in the world can't get that nagging voice out of our head that we just don't measure up. This can spill over to relationships, of course, when we get hung up on those issues to the detriment of ourselves, our marriage, and our intimacy. If we feel like we should have sex only in complete darkness because we're hung up about our butt, we're likely to turn down a lot of opportunities to connect with our spouses (and they probably think our tush is just fine anyway).

After all, how many times have you looked at a picture of yourself from ten years ago and thought, "Wow, I looked really good!" and you can't believe you were beating yourself up at the time feeling like a dumpy reject because of some perceived flaw? Does anyone really think, "When I lose ten pounds or get rid of this pooch, I'll want to have sex with my husband"? Let me save you some time, sit-ups and Weight Watchers points, girls, *you won't.* And here is the thing about turning forty or forty-five or even fifty, I've concluded: In some ways my best days of *looking good* are behind me, but my best days of *feeling good* are ahead of me. I am more comfortable with how my life is turning out and I'm happy with most of the decisions I've made, including having daily intimacy with Brad. And this allows me to be more confident in who I am.

Attraction is a mysterious thing–what draws one person to another enough to decide to date or to take the plunge and marry? I think there's something in our genetic wiring that makes us find one person desirable over another. One Friday night, Brad and I went out to dinner and were seated next to another couple. As you do, you notice people and we noticed them. He was very handsome, but she was only marginally pretty. Brad claimed they contradicted the "Law of Twos." Brad developed the "Law of Twos" many years ago, before we dated, when he was out in the world, surveying the bar scene with his friends. It is based on the premise that everyone rates on an attractiveness scale from one to ten, and that you cannot date or marry someone greater or lesser than two points. If you do? Hello heartache, angst, and disappointment. So a seven can date a nine or a five, but not a four.

True, variables can impact ratings–so an average guy with money might rank higher as might a cute gal with an outstanding sense of humor. Likewise a pretty girl with a horrible attitude might rank a point or two lower than expected, and a vapid stud could fall off the scale completely. Either way, it all balances out–we are attracted to and should pursue folks who fall into our general parameters of attractiveness. So I would say that the guy next to us was an eight, but she was just a five. And Brad and I speculated, and placed tacky odds and assumed that she must have one heck of a personality or that he must be a real dud.

There are plenty of men that I find attractive, but there are few that I'm attracted to–a fact for which my husband is thankful, I'm sure. I bring this up because as I age–getting both older and wiser, I hope–it's an important distinction. I saw this amazing documentary on PBS regarding the human face and the fact that there is a universal definition of outward beauty, which is symmetry. Apparently, people with symmetrical features are unanimously attractive, no matter what ethnicity. Certain specifications apply–the nose has a certain breadth and the chin has a certain shape and so on. Symmetry is harder to come by than you might think.

But what I'm talking about is the total package: Beyond looks, personality of course comes into play in the attraction game. Sometimes attraction comes from an amazing sense of confidence that one is attractive, despite whatever rank on a scale. Back in college, there was a girl named Jenna, who always had guys knocking at her door, mooning over her. My friends and I were flummoxed. How was Jenna getting these guys to fall for her? Don't get me wrong, she was pretty all right . . . and smart . . . and athletic . . . and (gasp) really quite nice. But she wasn't prettier than some of my friends who ended up alone in their dorm room in a pair of sweats with a bag of Cheetos, watching *Knots Landing*. There was not a fraternity cocktail or formal to which Jenna didn't receive at least one invitation (and sometimes two). She was The Perfect Date and was revered by boys and adored by girls.

What was her secret? The Cheetos-eaters were demanding to know. Why her and not us? After many impassioned discussions, we decided it was because she had self-confidence in spades, along with a touch of authentic nonchalance. The fact that she didn't necessarily care that boys were falling all over her made them do just that. She didn't obsess about boys, talk about boys, or seem to think about boys all that much. Better yet, she didn't obsess about herself, talk about herself, or overly focus on herself. She was just as happy to go to the movies with the girls as to go to her third cocktail party that month. Regardless of the company, she was comfortable in her own flawless

Ivory Girl skin and it showed. If she could bottle that and sell it, she would be a rich, rich woman.

It seems like just yesterday I was in those college sweats, but alas, there comes a time for us all when we have to acknowledge that the days of pulling our hair into a ponytail, throwing on jeans and a T-shirt, and running out the door without a trace of foundation are over. If that is still all it takes for you, well, then I'm happy not to know you, thanks, but your day will come, too. Now I have to take the time to look presentable . . . my mother would be so pleased. I'm nearly forty and she is *still* making helpful suggestions on clothes, hair, shoes, and overall presentation like "Remember, jeans aren't for everyone, dear." Clearly I didn't get the memo.

Standards of beauty have changed. When I was an adolescent, we reveled in new technology to make us prettier–like braces, contact lenses, and home perms. And fashion-wise, we all adored our Laura Ashley and Gunne Sax prairie dresses (which were long and billowy and very forgiving). But a whole new world has opened up in what is required for standard grooming, including facial waxing, self-tanners, and hair colorists. In this brave new world, grooming is king (or queen, depending on whom you ask). As my colorist recently asked me: "When are you going to love yourself enough to realize you need your hair colored every six weeks?" I guess I love myself enough to spend as much on my hair as I do on medical premiums . . .

I look at photos of my girlfriends and me from the late eighties and early nineties, and you know what sticks out the most to me? Our eyebrows–literally, they stick out! Nearly every one of us had big, bushy, overgrown eyebrows. This was before waxing and eyebrow grooming became essentials, and we knew no better than the accidental Brooke Shields look. Even my girlfriends who don't have excessive hair still had untamed brows and it showed. So there is a new norm and that norm is not unibrow or spiky brows or brows that leak into your eyeballs. I'm sorry, you can't change that. The new paradigm is well-groomed brows. Even for men.

I can't ignore these new standards. I know that my gray is growing in faster than the speed of light. I know that my eyebrows really do need to be combed, if you can believe it. And as my mother says, I "have to work hard to make my clothes look nice," which is code for I have to work hard to avoid the forty-year-old frumpy look. It's a huge challenge to have laundered, freshly pressed clothes that look nice and hang well when you're rushing kids off to school, swinging by the store on your way to work, and hoping that folks in your client meeting won't notice you haven't washed your hair since Tuesday. Sometimes I tire of having to take the time (which is still much less time than I spent coiffing during my high school days), but when I'm paying attention, it seems to pay off . . . at least when my mother visits.

So in order for me to present well, I require a daily shower (sometimes two) and aggressive facial waxing. It's no longer "pretty is as pretty does." It's now "pretty is as good as your Personal Grooming Budget." (By the way, I am now on a payment plan with my hair colorist.) It's fascinating to look at any "A List" starlet in Hollywood today and realize that this starlet is probably no prettier than most of my girlfriends from college.

She has a lot of cash. She probably has a personal trainer, a personal chef, a personal stylist, a personal yoga instructor, a great plastic surgeon (oh, come on, haven't you noticed?), a personal colorist, a personal esthetician (today's starlets have *no* body hair, I tell you–when did this become mandatory?), a famous hairdresser, and fantastically stylish friends.

Now, based on all that, don't you think she should look slam damn fabulous? And I can name ten girls right now who are "wake up, roll outta bed" prettier than her any day. In fact, we can name a dozen other Hollywood gazillionaire starlets who, thanks to impeccable grooming, have gone from "just aw-right" to "who is that stunning creature?" Gone are the days when gorgeous, genetically gifted creatures like Liz Taylor, Marilyn Monroe, and Grace Kelly got by without personal trainers, all-over body waxing, and a cadre of personal assistants. They had natural beauty. Now such looks can be plucked, squeezed, and styled right into you, and thanks to PhotoShop and soft-focus lenses, even an average girl can be turned into the latest diva, if she gets lucky.

As a result, I have a dirty little secret. Actually, I have many, but this one I'm willing to share. I am a *People* magazine junkie–I actually get it *in the mail.* I can't even pretend it's an impulse purchase in the "10 items or less" lane. I subscribe and pay to receive a weekly fix of Hollywood crack. And many of my friends do, too. Except for my brilliant sister-in-law, the investment banker. She is hard-core, and has graduated from *People* magazine to *Us*. "I just want the dirt on celebs, I don't care about all those feel-good stories about people who lost 200 pounds or save seals for a living."

People comes on Saturday and it takes me only twenty minutes to scan my version of crack from cover to cover, but I can track the befores and afters, the breakups and the affairs, the rehabbers and the outright losers. And although the Hollywood lifestyle is not attainable to us plain folk, I am still hooked. Because in the golden days of Hollywood, we were infatuated with an idea of beauty and glamour that we could never have. But today, we are infatuated by the accessibility of that beauty and glamour. Because, if she can look that beautiful after a little waxing, exercising, implants, hair coloring, and teeth whitening, can't I?

So, yeah, sometimes I wonder how I would look in size 6 designer jeans (dare to dream, right?) or whether hair extensions could change my life (and I am most certain they would). But at the end of the day, every day, I am intimate with my husband, and that is most important to my body image. And who knew that would be such a boost? Not me, friends. Knowing that I can connect with my husband in an intimate and meaningful way makes me feel good . . . and him, too, I might add. Because having sexual confidence makes you feel more confident in the world. Who doesn't want to go out into the world knowing that somebody would like to get their groove on with you? So do people who have sex a lot feel sexier? For me, sometimes! Two months into this arrangement, I am happier and more content in my marriage than ever before, and that makes me feel pretty and great.

As I'm soon turning forty, I'm realizing that many things my mother has told me are–gasp–really true. These nuggets include the fact that Mother Nature marches on, and she doesn't slow down for anyone. Not that it matters all that much. Everyone can get plastic surgery–it's no longer for the rich and famous. You can go off to Costa Rica and "spa" with your girlfriends and arrive home looking years younger (after the bruising and swelling go down, of course), or take out a three-year finance plan–just like a car–to fund that Botox and face-lift.

Plastic surgery is *everywhere*–advertisements on TV, on billboards, on every magazine for women. I can't imagine I'll be immune to the pull of "a little work." I don't need a new chin, or new boobs, or a weirdly stiff forehead. But I might need a little bit here and little nudge there, and who will know? I think that the working mom/stay-at-home debate of my generation is going to morph into the "to have a little work" or "not have a little work" debate as we age. You heard it here first, girls. We're going to have finally sorted through our stuff about how to best raise our kids and then, poof, we're old and wrinkled and we're going to war over plastic surgery–sin or savior? Like before, we'll devour each other until we get it right. There will come a day when plastic surgery is the norm and some poor soul (very possibly me) opts out, and is forever the odd gal out.

Brad claims he will never, ever support me having "a little work." It's not because he's cheap. Apparently, he likes me just the way I am. On one level, that is very sweet. On the other, very naïve. "What if I look fifty and all my friends look forty because they had work done?" I wail. "Does it really matter how good I look if they've ruined the curve?"

"I don't care what everyone looks like. I married you because I think you're beautiful," he responds. "Why would I endorse you changing that?"

"Well, because no one can tell the future and I could be quite unbeautiful in my later years. I wouldn't be changing who I am, I would only be doing some slight tweaking. What's so bad about that?"

But Brad can really shut down the debate when he references our daughter. "What will she think if she sees her mother conforming to these bizarre societal standards? What are you teaching her when you care about all that stuff?" I sigh heavily. He's right, I know. I do struggle with raising a daughter in a world that puts such a bizarre premium on outward looks. And I want her to be so bright and fantastically confident that she oozes pretty from the inside. So I do worry about that. But really, do I have to tell her anything, especially if Mommy went on a little spa trip to Costa Rica? After all, the key to "a little work" is that it's so good that no one really knows . . .

Certainly there is something to be said for self-improvement–where do you think this crazy idea of having sex with my husband every day for a year came from? But I am at a place where, paunchy tummy and crow's feet aside, I'm okay with me. This may be a gift of age and experience and being in a great and supportive relationship. Because my husband likes me, too, apparently. While my figure was never my strongest suit, I have a great smile and good hair. And over time I have come to accept my flaws and embrace my strengths. It helps to have a spouse who does the same on my behalf.

So I am Every Gal. And in some ways being Every Gal has

been great–I'm an average woman having daily intimacy with the man I have vowed to try to like forever. Sometimes I don't shave my legs; sometimes I have stinky breath. But I'm still hanging in there. So, if this is not a destination, but a journey–there is no time like the present for intimacy. I suspect those unbelievably sexy Victoria's Secret models don't have more sex than the rest of us, so score one for the girls who can't sashay down a runway in front of thirty million people in their underwear and be happy about it. The great thing about sexual intimacy is that it's egalitarian–it transcends class, race, and certainly the high-fashion definition of beauty and attractiveness. There are only two people who have to agree on sexy–in this case, Brad and his wife.

Most of my friends are now off the market and happily married and the rest pretend they're happily married, at least for a few hours on a Friday night. And while there are plenty of attractive people in the bunch, there's no one for whom I'd swap Brad. To some that might sound obsequious, but in reality, it's a bit selfish. Here is a guy who does it for me in the looks department . . . and the brains department, and the integrity department, and the dad department, and so on. And most important, he knows how to be married to me. Is he perfect? Absolutely not. But neither are all the other guys out there that fit my bill of tall, dark, and handsome (all things Brad is, in my book).

I asked Brad about it and hoped he felt the same way about me: "I know plenty of women who are attractive, but none of them offer me anything that I don't already have."

I'll thank my hair stylist tomorrow for that.

SEPTEMBER

It's Hard to Feel Sexy in a Suburban (But It's Way Better than a Minivan)

The back door opened and I heard Brad come in. His footsteps echoed down the hall.

"Hey, honey, I'm back here!" I called out. "Come on back. How was your day?"

He entered the bedroom and I heard him rustling around in his closet, hanging up his belt, and tossing his shoes into the back of the closet. "It was fine. Where are you anyway?" he asked.

"I'm in the tub. The kids are upstairs with a video. I have a cold beer here, too . . . Want to join me?"

He said, "No, you go on and finish up. I'm fine."

I don't even know where to begin with this one.

It's Friday night and we're scheduled to go out. I have strategically placed the kids upstairs to watch a video. Here I am trying, really *trying*, to create some moments that stand out from our standard sex-every-day moments and this is all I get? The disappointment is exacerbated by the fact that we have the most awesome garden tub in our master bathroom. In fact, when we first looked at this house, we were blown away by the indulgent bathroom–double vanity, tiled shower, and a tub *à deux* that sits in the corner. It was a far cry from our teeny master bathroom in our old house (which didn't really qualify as a master bath because it was attached to another bedroom).

This tub is like a small swimming pool, and when we first moved in, we took baths whenever we could and our kids bathed nightly. It was like Spa Muller. While we had visited lots of places with nice bathtubs, we had never *owned* such a spectacular bathing experience. Then we got our first water bill and it was like four hundred bucks! Our waterlogged eyes couldn't believe it when we read the bill, but I guess it makes sense. We were filling a tub the size of a plastic pool from Wal-Mart–and nearly every day. From then on, we went on a tub rationing program. Our kids learned to take showers and we doled out tub time for special occasions and as a reward for good behavior.

So when I was inviting Brad to join me, it was a twofer–we were going out (a regular and always welcome occurence) and I was rewarding myself for a job well done in the domestic goddess department (still kind of a new thing even after two months). After all, I thought I was doing a darn admirable job on our intimacy arrangement by getting the kids all happy and situated upstairs, while I was ready and waiting inside this glorious tub. All this, and some friskiness, too, was lost on Brad.

Later I told him. "You know, I was trying to mix things up a bit with the bath and beer thing. I'm talking two kinds of suds involved. I can't believe you weren't even interested. I mean, can you throw me a bone?"

"Whoops–I totally missed the signals, sweetie." He grimaced, embarrassed. "I'm sorry. If I had known this was a planned rec activity, I would have been more involved. I guess I'm kinda used to our routine."

Routines. They're a curse and a blessing.

We had gotten into a lovin' groove–occasionally in the A.M., but nearly always in the P.M. On the weekend, we would mix it into our "getting ready to go out" repertoire. This caused Brad to be a completely charming dinner guest because he was so darned slap happy, and I could grossly overeat and overdrink and nose-dive into a catatonic sleep at the end of the evening, because our little intimacy engagement was behind us. But the bathtub? Clearly, I had thrown him off with a change of venue.

It's September and the early-morning routine is back in high gear: Wake up at dawn, shower, wake up the children, get lunches made, backpacks found, children dressed, teeth brushed, and off to school. As I see my own children hustle off to school and I walk to the end of the driveway to grab the paper, it hits me that I'm the *mom* here. It's not *me* skipping off to school with nary a trouble in the world. Instead, I realize that I have ahead of me years and years of this routine. *Years and years.*

It's a whirlwind, but by 7:45, the house is quiet again; I'm frazzled and popping open my second Diet Coke of the morning. I'm taking comfort in that soft fizzing noise and thinking about the old days, when I was a young and single marketing executive, living in the big city. On the weekend, I could sleep in until eleven, eat lunch at three in the afternoon, take *hours* to get dressed for the evening, and then cap it all off by watching cheesy Lifetime movies until the wee hours of the morning. Fast-forward five years . . .

"Hello. Charla Muller," I answered into the phone, a pencil wedged in my teeth.

"Hey, it's Nina, how are you?" Nina was calling me from home.

"Ugh. I'm so tired I could die. I just went and napped in the handicapped stall. I don't know what's wrong with me. Hang on . . . I need to put my head between my legs, I'm feeling woozy."

"Well, it's two P.M. Have you eaten?"

"What? No, not really. I don't feel good. Don't really have an appetite." I was reduced to mumbling by this point.

"Char, are you sure you couldn't be pregnant?"

That woke me up. "Don't be ridiculous! I couldn't be pregnant—it's too soon. Heck, we're still waiting for our wedding album from the photographer."

"I want you to go eat a pack of Nabs from the vending machine and go by Eckerd on the way home for a pregnancy test."

Whoops.

Yep, within ninety days of getting married, Brad and I were actually pregnant. So after a lovely courtship, wonderful engagement, and dream wedding: Hello! You're pregnant, Charla! No, we didn't plan to get pregnant this quickly, we thought it would take some time, but it turns out I'm *very* fertile.

But we were incredibly excited, and had fluffy dreams of cuddling together alongside the beautiful sleeping baby, and moving her into a decked-out nursery that would make Martha Stewart weep with joy. Those dreams were swiftly shoved aside by the sloppy realization of what it means to be parents to a real-live baby. I mean, it's *alive* and everything!

Don't get me wrong. This is what I wanted. Or what I thought I wanted–in the abstract. And that's what the future is most of the time–a dreamy, vague notion of some sort. For me, I wanted to get married. I wanted to have kids. I wanted to work–a little (I didn't want to be CEO, but I did want to be successful). I wanted to live in a great house in a great neighborhood and go to fabulous dinner parties every weekend where I would mingle with my charming, witty, and wildly successful friends.

It's only when you look into the shadows of those dreams that you see the sharp and pointy details of your future. Of living with a spouse who isn't perpetually in a good mood (has he always been this grumpy?). Of raising babies who don't want to sleep (from *whose* gene pool is this kid?). Of living with neighbors who are just as bleary-eyed as you are, and not nearly as charming as you had hoped (like you, they were so much fun before kids).

Once our children debuted, the impact they had on our sex lives was significant. We went from lovely sex several times a week to . . . [insert chirping cricket noises here]. So while I was aware of the drastic change in our sex life, it was trumped by this *amazing brand-new human life!* Nothing was more important than keeping alive this small person who weighed only nine pounds. Nine pounds?! You have no idea how small and fragile babies are, and how many things can go wrong with small and fragile babies–it's enough to haunt you in your sleep. Which it does–all the time–to first-time mothers. I briefly worried, in between all the other worries that I had as a new mother, whether this was a blip on the sex screen or whether, after I finally let the dust settle around the last box of Huggies, this was going to be a permanent state of affairs.

My sense of desirability went bye-bye after I had a baby. A few moments that led me down into the valley of Motherhood, as a friend so astutely observed, included: when the ladies at the Lancôme counter started to call me "ma'am"; when my hairdresser threw up his hands and announced, "I'm at a complete loss to help you"; when I realized that I'm no longer the "young hotshot" at work; when my husband asked me if women think Angelina Jolie is as hot as men do (the answer is yes); and when my need for sleep grew exponentially greater than my need for sex.

Yes, the list is tediously long. But there's one moment that confirmed just how much I had changed in the last few years and how unglamorous and unsexy I had become:

I'm driving down the street and listening to Anita Baker's "Giving You the Best That I Got," which is a languorously sexy song. Sadly, it does not occur to me that the song has absolutely no relevance to me, Brad, or my sex life. Rather, I am basking in the sun, the kids are at preschool, and I'm thrilled that I don't have to listen to Radio Disney. I am happy, relaxed, and feeling good. The window is down and I have on some *très* trendy sunglasses. I might even have managed to slap on some lip gloss, making it a banner day. I pull up to a stoplight, and see a cute, sharply dressed, sexy man sitting in a luxury car next to me. I wonder about him, and whether he would think I might be remotely cute, and I smile nonchalantly and dreamily (disinterested, of course, because I am a happily married woman . . . who's now intimate every day with her husband, too!), but I like to think that maybe, just maybe, on this breezy day in September, I've still got it. That perhaps I can be married, a mother of two, and still be attractive to men.

And then I realize, I *don't* still got it. That in reality, I am towering over this attractive man, looking *down* into his luxury BMW from the great height of my monster, Mom-sized SUV. And that I and my two booster seats and my crapload of Happy Meals toys, chewed-up crayons, socks, cat fur, hair bows, and "artwork" from last year don't really cut it. It was a disconcerting realization that I had sitting up high in my ungainly SUV that gets about twelve miles to the gallon. I scrunched down in my seat and changed the station to clear my head of the shocking awkwardness of it all.

However, I will say this: I don't care how ridiculous and unsexy I felt at that moment in my big, honkin' SUV, because at least I will not ever, *ever* drive a minivan. I don't care how practical they are, how highly rated they are, how great the resale value is, how the children enjoy their bucket seats and never fight anymore, and how all the electronics are wired up to each seat. It does not matter that my trendy, quite handsome younger brother drives one and constantly taunts me to "come over to the Dark Side" with his GPS system, iPod-infused, DVD-playing, bucket-seated, great mileage minivan. I simply can't. It's a flagrant, open, "shout out to the world" admission that I am no longer relevant, stylish, sexy, or cute.

There are too many other things I have in my life that shout out that I am no longer relevant, stylish, sexy, or cute, so I'm hanging on to my boat on wheels. And my girls in the minivans? We'll, they're just as sold on their wheels as I am on mine, and hey, I guess even Angelina Jolie could look hot driving a minivan. I would rather drive a luxury BMW (and they don't make minivans, so don't you think that means something?). And for you hybrid-loving sisters out there getting all worked up about my monthly gas intake, don't worry about me. I make up for it in other ways–I *occasionally* recycle and *occasionally* use paper instead of plastic and have been known to buy in bulk, *on occasion.* Baby steps . . .

But I am never just occasionally more interesting without my children–I am *always* more interesting without them. Don't get me wrong: I love my children . . . dearly. I think they are nearly perfect and the thought that I can't even begin to know all the ways in which I am scarring and disappointing them for life keeps me up at night; it really does. But the fact remains, I am much more fun and entertaining without them. And you really don't know and appreciate that until they're here, and then it's too late and you're stuck lugging around a diaper bag the size of a Mini-Cooper and wondering if today is the day your kid will get head lice at preschool.

A lovely couple we know just put in a pool in their backyard. The husband wanted to have a giant pool party for families. The wife wanted to have a small, intimate pool party for couples. Husband thinks said pool party with fourteen adults and twenty children sounds like "great fun." The wife doesn't. "We'll all be in the pool playing games, hanging out, having a cocktail . . . it'll be great," he says. "Charla, what do you think?"

Is he kidding? First, there is not one wife in that bunch who will be in that pool "playing games, hanging out, and having a cocktail." After forty and motherhood, it's simply not a good look for many. And after you get out of the pool wringing wet and it's time for dinner? Again, not a good look for most. Hanging out drinking in a pool was so Spring Break 1989 (and need I mention that no one had kids on Spring Break 1989?).

Second, the husbands will be standing *near* but not in the pool, playing games (like placing bets on when some cute wife is going to hop out of her Lilly cover-up and go for a dip) and having cocktails. Meanwhile the wives hump it to feed the kids hot dogs, wipe up spilled lemonade, get more butter for the corn on the cob, and generally work themselves into such a sweat that they'll wish they could jump into the pool and cool off. Or at least they'll consider the pool a sad alternative to the chaos of feeding twenty children.

And then, once the kids are fed and swimming in the pool, you cannot even consider having a meaningful adult conversation because the odds are that you'll find yourself totally distracted. It's highly likely you won't be able to make eye contact with an adult because you'll be looking over the shoulder of some friend of a friend that you're talking to. Let's imagine: As you're engaging "Mike, the New Guy from the bank," you can't help but watch someone else's kid standing in the distance and sticking his arm down the drain hole of the pool. And you're nodding your head as "Mike, the New Guy from the bank" talks about how much he and his wife love their new house, and you're thinking about how this kid's arm is going to get stuck, and you're wondering if butter or Crisco will work better to unstick that dumb kid's arm.

You just know how the pool party would unfold if this couple decided to invite parents *and* children.

So *puuuullllleeeease*, let me pay twelve bucks an hour for a sitter, leave my kids at home, take a shower, and come to your house and drink lots and lots of your wine. I promise I will be charming, interested, and interesting. I will thank you profusely for inviting me and I will try to conduct myself in a manner that will get me invited back (no guarantees, though). I will look you in the eye and be fully engaged when we talk and I will not look over your shoulder and wonder if the kid who's got that chain link around his neck is going to get hurt and if his parents even know what he's doing.

So if people want to get the best that I, Charla, have to offer, then take me somewhere without my kids. And without other people's kids. I promise, it is then that "I'm giving you the best that I got."

Brad would agree. After all, some of the best intimacy we've ever had during the course of our entire marriage was when our children weren't around or we weren't around our children. "I don't understand it," Brad would exclaim. "That was great, why can't it be like that every day?"

Well, dream on, Dorothy. Most days we're *not* at a charming B&B where we can sleep till nine, have a leisurely breakfast, and stroll down a Main Street so perfect it seems straight out of central casting. And most days my children are *not* comfortably ensconced at my parents' house, where their every need is being met with great attentiveness. And most days I am *not* exempt from cooking, cleaning, and doing laundry. And most days I am *not* dressed in a cute, freshly pressed outfit that makes me look and feel fairly attractive. And most days I do *not* shower and get dressed while sipping a glass of perfect chardonnay for a romantic dinner prepared by someone who is not me.

So the lesson here is that real life rarely, if ever, is conducive to great intimacy. Rather, real life begets real sex. And sometimes real sex is a quickie. Sometimes it's a distracted roll in the hay. Real people having real intimacy while living real life is not always sexy. Rather, it's imperfect and muddled, just like real life.

Sadly, sometimes real life doesn't include any real intimacy at all. Many of my girlfriends have, once they have conceived the number of children they wanted to, turned their backs on their sperm donors (oops, I mean husbands) and are trying desperately to get out of ever having sex with them again. I was once among them. However, pre–The Gift, I was amenable to hopping back in the sack for an occasional shot at procreation. Women have an unbelievable biological drive for wanting babies that I could compare to men's unbelievable drive for wanting sex . . . or wanting insanely expensive cars. It's a powerful, powerful thing that is very difficult to turn off, even when you are in the midst of chaos with one kid just out of diapers, one baby still in them, and extrabig plastic toys and blocks scattered throughout your family room, which you can't imagine ever being tidy again. The need for a new baby, even with two perfectly good and wonderful children, supersedes the reality of my being stretched to the extreme.

"Oh, come on, honey, let's try for number three. It will be wonderful," I said on more than one occasion, pre–The Gift.

"Which part?" he asked. "The conceiving or the next eighteen years of raising a contributing member of society?"

Who was I kidding? Definitely the latter. "We would be great *with three kids. Besides," I reminded him, "you're one of three. Wasn't it great?"*

In reality for Brad, not really. According to him, he was stuck in the middle seat on all transcontinental car rides, where his father chain-smoked with the windows sealed shut. He was always the odd man out on the roller coaster. And if there was someone left out at cards, it was usually Brad. Oh, the list of "Third Child" transgressions goes on and on. But the real reason Brad didn't want three kids? He wanted his wife back.

Explain, *s'il vous plaît.*

Then the truth came out. He admitted that he thought, despite all my best efforts, being a mom and being a wife were at such odds that I defaulted to one. And guess what? It wasn't being a lovey-dovey, superattentive, "please, tell me all about your day while I rub your feet" kind of spouse (if ever such a woman existed, she certainly didn't exist in south Charlotte). I think what he really missed was the vibrant, engaged, and funny gal he married. The one who loved to try new restaurants, debate government policy, and watch late-night television in bed. The one who wanted to spend time with just him. In his defense, we didn't have much of a newlywed period. "I didn't get much of you before we had kids. If we keep having them, there won't be any time with you on the back end either. Our whole marriage will be about our kids. And as much as I love them, I love you and want to spend some portion of my life with the woman I married."

Wow. How does one formulate a cogent response to that, I ask? Deep down inside, I knew Brad was right–that while Baby No. 3 may have been right for me, it wasn't right for us. I would still float the perpetual "let's have another kid" platform and I still get pangs of regret and harbor hope that he might get some wild hair and change his mind. Which is ridiculous–wild hair and Brad go together about as well as Charla and small, yippy dogs, which is not at all.

So in some way, I was able to recognize that this somewhat new arrangement of daily intimacy was a nod to the fact that Brad missed me. That while it was too premature in the cycle of raising children to bring back the carefree, spontaneous woman I once was in her entirety, there were bits and pieces of her I could attempt to resurrect. I was coming out from the valley of early motherhood to a time when, as my children are now of school age, do not cling on to me every second. Gaining a portion of me back included having an active and fulfilling sex life . . . and no new babies. Was I sad? Sure, I still am sometimes, especially when I see a sweet, cuddly newborn. And most surely when I reflect on all the baby names I didn't get to use. But I couldn't compromise my relationship with Brad by coercing him into something that he didn't want. Besides, when this dream baby woke up screaming at 4 A.M. and Brad rolled over with a look that said, "This was Your idea: You get up!"–well, that was a situation I hoped mightily to avoid.

Folks can argue about who is best suited to lose this debate–the person who wants the baby or the person who doesn't. And while we each passionately defended our position, in reality, Brad was a tad more passionate about *not* having a third child than I was about having a third. We had two wonderful kids, and not having a third was not going to render me or our family incomplete. And in reality, I didn't want a third badly enough to take it all on myself. I wasn't one of those wives willing to shoulder any and all baby duties for the next eighteen years. I'm not a masochist for goodness' sake. So I did defer on this one, which, all told, was pretty amazing for Big Idea Girl.

On occasion, I still lay my head on Brad's shoulder and murmur about how sweet a third would have been, how old he or she would be now if we had gone ahead and done it. How wonderful our older children would be with the third. But it's all just that . . . sweet nothings about something that will never happen. Because if our baby-making days weren't officially behind us, I couldn't appreciate all the gifts that this next phase will bring, namely a growing back together of sorts. That, and of raising kids who can finally bathe, feed, and dress themselves, for example. In a nutshell, kids who can do that miracle of modern humans: multitask!

"So how was your day, sweetie?"

Brad replied with an "Mmmmm . . ."

"Our son's teacher called, he's doing really well in preschool, no more notes home in his book bag. Isn't that great?"

Brad, again, managed an "Uh-hmm."

"So, can we talk about that weekend at the lake? I think it would be fun, don't you think? We could have cocktails on the boat and then go out for a nice dinner, it's supposed to be great weather."

Brad finally had had enough. "I'm sorry, but are we really talking about this stuff now*? It's not very sexy."*

"Oops, sorry. Keep going."

I didn't start out as an intimacy multitasker, but necessity demanded that I try it. And after many years of juggling the world of Mullers, I became quite good at it. However, I soon learned that our daily trysts couldn't handle multitasking, nor did it need it.

In my husband's view, sex is serious business and one should stay focused on the task at hand. And in the old days, I would have agreed wholeheartedly. You could have bet your birthday money that I would never, ever get chatty on my husband. We both treated the anomaly of intimacy with great reverence.

But I feel this great need to talk to him during the deed. Perhaps it's my wiring–this was, after all, a time to bond with him and we all know how women bond: talk, talk, talk. Also, while you can't physically multitask during sex (at least I can't clean the tile in the bathroom and get it on with my husband), you can mentally multitask. Guys brush their teeth and pee at the same time, so why, I reasoned, can't I have sex and talk about whether Janine is really a competent babysitter or if we need to branch out?

Well, because it's distracting, and concentration is involved, at least on a man's part. Me? Well, remember that I was trying to multitask . . . so I'm not exerting too much mental energy on my end. You can't blame a girl for trying. After all, school is in full swing now, and I've got a little alone time with my husband, and I want to make the most of it. What I failed to realize is that in some ways I was connecting with my husband on his "turf," not mine. Granted, intimacy was a common experience to us both, but the connection that we experienced was, for him, far superior to any other form of communication–my blabbing on and on about something, his BlackBerry, the newspaper, or even television. I needed to simply shut my mouth and let him enjoy this intimate communiqué. He didn't feel the need to chitchat and neither should I. Sometimes intimacy with your spouse requires no embellishments.

With our everyday model came some guy stuff that I had not considered, since I'm not a guy and all. For example, my husband can always rise to the occasion, but he does not always close the deal (apologies for the bad metaphors, but they do the job). There were days when he had to call it a day. Normally, my husband (and most men living on this planet) would be appalled and embarrassed by the idea that they couldn't deliver the goods. Certainly it's an important, if not tangible, commentary on one's sexual prowess. But when you're living in a new sex paradigm, things indeed shift. My husband was having sex every day, with no strings attached, mind you. So apparently if there was an occasional glitch, it was no biggie.

"Uh, sorry, but I think this is it," he said one night.

"What? You're not going to finish?" I was incredulous . . . and alarmed.

"Hon, we've been doing this for nearly eighty-eight straight days . . . I don't have it in me. There is nothing left, and I mean that literally."

I wanted to be an appropriately sympathetic wife, and I was sure that this would be a blow to his manhood. "Oh, honey, I'm so sorry. It's okay . . . really . . . are you okay?"

"Of course, I'm fine. I think I'll just watch some *Sports Center* if that's okay with you."

"Wow, I must say that you're really handling this well," I finally offered.

He smiled serenely, rolled over, and countered, "Well, there's always tomorrow."

And that was a little gift of The Gift. Brad knew he was going to have sex every day no matter what, so it took the pressure off having sex perfectly every time. He still wanted intimacy, mind you, and still enjoyed it. But if he couldn't close the deal, it wasn't like some missed opportunity that wouldn't roll around again until another lunar eclipse. No, we both had a nice connection, participated in a warm and intimate moment, and to quote Scarlet O'Hara, "Tomorrow is another day."

Every new day brought various challenges to our schedule, and so we hustled and negotiated and got in a routine with our kids, too. We started distracting them so we could go distract ourselves.

We insisted on strict bedtimes. As a kindergarten teacher so sagely told me, "If your six-year-old knows the plot of *Desperate Housewives*, he is not getting enough sleep." Babies, toddlers, and middle-schoolers all need adequate sleep—even in the summer and on weekends. Honestly, having sex at midnight when I'm bone tired after a day of work, carpooling, changing diapers, and cooking dinner is *not* my idea of a good time. But a romp in the hay between 7 and 10 P.M. is really quite preferred and also energizing.

We didn't allow co-sleeping. And we weren't afraid to close our bedroom door and lock it. And I reminded myself that kids are never too young to learn the meaning of a closed door, and to exercise the discipline not to open it. I know finding fifteen uninterrupted minutes in the course of the day is virtually impossible, but a locked door will at least buy you a few.

And we found ourselves an amazing babysitter, whom the children run to in excitement upon her arrival, which zaps the guilt right out of going out for date nights. I know a woman who did not leave her first child alone with anybody for an entire year. She never once went out with her husband for dinner, or a movie, or even a cup of coffee. Okay, I'm not trying to be critical, but she's not really going to win any awards with that one, especially "Wife of the Year." But that's beside the point. Because first of all, who is to say that I was up for Wife of the Year? Although I think my effort should count for something–don't you?

As much as I hate to admit it, television and videos can be your friends, and we became especially tight with Señor TV and Madame Video during this year of The Gift. We weren't afraid to park a kid or two in front of a video for a while because, in the end, everyone would walk away happier. And honestly, we're better parents when we have some time together alone.

As I became a more experienced mother, I knew when to ask for help when I needed it. After my first cesarean, I cried with joy when I left the hospital. "Let my wonderful life as Mother to the World's Most Perfect Baby begin!" I proclaimed to the world as I stepped (or rather was wheeled) into the bright light of a July day. After my second cesarean, I cried with sadness when they finally kicked me out of the lovely room on maternity row where nice-enough nurses brought me my baby every three hours and asked me if I'd had a BM yet (the answer was no, of course). But this time, I left armed. I grabbed all the giant maxipads, several pairs of the giant, weirdly stretchy disposable underwear, a cotton baby blanket (they were so soft!), and a handful of stool softeners. Yes, this time I was prepared, right down to The Conspiracy.

The Conspiracy was not my idea. It was that of my girlfriends. In fact, I had no idea it existed until they spilled the beans. "So, don't forget, get the doc to write you a note regarding sex," one said as she reviewed with me her checklist. "What kind of note?" I asked, truly and deeply ignorant. "Well, you're not supposed to have sex for a while after the baby is born, and I always ask my ob-gyn to write a note to tack on a few weeks for good measure."

"Tell me more," I begged another friend in on The Conspiracy.

"Well," this one continued, "if a baby has ripped you from sunup to sundown, and it's unlikely you'll have a pain-free bowel movement until the next full moon, you might need a few extra weeks of R&R. Just don't let on to your husband when things are getting back to normal. It's important that you act as disappointed as he about this 'restriction.' " Ah, let the games begin. And so began my career of dodging sex with my nice husband.

Fast forward, and here we are, trying to weave intimacy back into the grind of everyday family life. Although it pains me to think of it, I can't help but compare our new arrangement to a story involving my grandmother. She had only one travel dream–a trip to the Holy Land. This was to be her only trip abroad, and possibly her only trip outside the Southeast. When she arrived home from the Holy Land, she made a big to-do about each of us grandchildren sitting by her on the couch to look through all 1,437 photos made with her Kodak Brownie.

"And this is me on a camel! Can you beleeeve it?" she squealed.

"That's nice, Ma. Your pantsuit seemed to wear well while you were over there."

"Oooh, honey. It did. It did. And this is the River Jordan."

"Really?" I asked. I pulled the album closer. "It's kind of dark and murky looking."

And it was, dark, murky looking . . . and very creepy.

"You should know that this is the most important river that ever was . . . In fact, I got baptized in the River Jordan while I was over there!" Ma said.

"Are you telling me you waded out into that dark cold river and got baptized again, Ma?"

"I sure did. And I have got the picture to prove it."

She flipped ahead to the picture of her standing in the River Jordon. I held the album close and peered intently to get a good look. Having come from a long line of God-fearing Baptists, we are familiar with total-immersion baptism. My mother was baptized in a river when she was young and I was baptized (in our church's baptismal pool) when I was twelve.

"Ma, is that you . . . the one with the giant flowery shower cap?"

"That's me! Have you just seen nothing like it?"

Well, she was right, I have seen nothing like my grandmother standing in the River Jordan in the deeply spiritual ritual of baptismal immersion wearing a giant, plastic flowery shower cap from the CVS.

"Ma, what do you have on your head and why?"

"It's a shower cap! Anyone knows that you can't get a shampoo and set in the Holy Land. I had to make my hairdo last ten whole days and I tell you it was not easy!"

And right she was. Even in the most special moments, there is a thread of practicality. And in some ways, you can enjoy those spiritual moments more if you're prepared. Just like my grandmother did. This has never been truer than when it comes to dealing with real life, real schedules, and real intimacy. Grabbing a special moment in the chaos of every day with Brad takes some preparation. And no, we don't do it wearing flowery shower caps.

So the homework is done, the kids are asleep, and we've used up our water quota for the month. But the truth is that this space, this home, is just as meaningful to me as the River Jordan is to my grandmother. This is where it all happens. As sociable as I am, it's the journeys that Brad and I have taken and will continue to take as a couple and as parents–warming up bottles, cheering our babies' first steps, teaching them how to read–that are the greatest road we'll ever take. Maybe we did miss out on a longer newlywed period because of the swift arrivals of our children, but this is where we are. I see Brad noodling on the computer. I put my hand on his shoulder, and give him a tap.

OCTOBER

Work, Work, Work

"Hey, hon!" I yelled out, hearing Brad come through the door.

"Hey, how was your day?" Brad asked.

"It was fine, but work was a drag. Listen, we've got to be at the Fullers' at seven, and the kids will be home from a playdate any minute. I'm gonna fold a quick load of clothes, and then let's go ahead and knock out some L-O-V-E before all the chaos. You game?"

"I'm on my way!" Brad called back.

"Love you," I said.

"Love you, too."

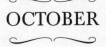

I never dreamed I'd pencil in on my calendar a daily tryst with Brad: 2 P.M.–Conference call. 3 P.M.–Carpool to dance, pop by bank, and run in grocery store on the way home. 4 P.M.–Meet exterminator, check e-mail, pay a few bills online, and throw clothes in dryer. 5 P.M.–Start dinner, manage homework, sign permission slips, check e-mail, prep for PTA meeting, and locate missing cat, Merlin. 6:30 P.M.–leave for PTA meeting; from car call sitter about tomorrow's schedule, call mother, and call best friend in New Jersey. 8 P.M.–Nice little Gift with Brad. 9 P.M.–Fold clothes, wash face, brush teeth, read a few chapters of book for Book Club.

Prekids, Brad and I worked together at the same company, and it was all good. We could commiserate about the office, tag team on project deadlines and client demands, and swap gossip from the same watercooler. Our roles weren't all that different–we were both working spouses–and we had plenty of time for each other and for our schedule. But now that Brad is the full-time working dad of two, and I'm the part-time working mom of two who is also managing most of the house, our paths have diverged. And with this divergence of our schedules, our perspectives have changed, too. While we would both say our family is our priority, Brad's career has moved front and center as he is now the major breadwinner, and with the addition of our kids, our to-do list has quadrupled and our ideas about sharing new responsibilities were initially blown to bits.

Most marriages start out with having to make adjustments–the wife may be a morning person, and her husband may be a night owl, or the wife is fastidiously tidy, and her husband doesn't mind leaving dirty dishes in the sink overnight. One may feel the need to unload a clean dishwasher right away and the other may simply pull out clean dishes on demand. These differences start as novelties, all part of the "to know you is to love you" process. But sometimes those differences can morph into "to know you is to wonder how it cannot *occur* to you to take out the garbage when it is overflowing banana peels and leaking a small puddle of nasty ooze onto the floor!" These are the things that can gnaw at a relationship. Throw a couple of Brand-New Human Lives into the mix, and you get a chronic, sweaty tug-of-war over power in marriage–who makes the decisions about the kids, money, sex–you name it. Let the fun begin.

Things were easier for my parents' generation. Dad had a successful career, and Mom did a great job raising us. (Look, Mom, I'm writing a book–yeah, it's about That Which Shall Remain Nameless.) He had his gig and she had hers–the boundaries and responsibilities were pretty clear. My mother handled everything at home, and my father worked on building a business. The fact that my mother was incredibly competent at most all things domestic was both a blessing and a curse for my father. She kept the house; she fixed electronics and small appliances; she sewed and mended (and in the seventies had a very unfortunate run-in with macramé); she landscaped and on occasion kept a garden. Mom tidied, organized, and rearranged; she killed snakes and fumigated hornets' nests, decorated on a budget and later without one . . . There was nothing in our house that my mother couldn't handle, couldn't figure out how to handle, or didn't know whom to call to handle. Oh yeah, and she raised my brother and me (and Dad did, too, of course, and was always present at all our landmark events).

When I was growing up, if my dad knew where the toolbox in our house was located, it would have been a surprise to me . . . and to my mother. Mom was not a wilting flower–both by design (she came from hardy stock) and demand (if she didn't know how to do it, fix it, or make it, it was not going to get done, fixed, or made). My mother would have made a killer executive or an electrical engineer . . . or as we've discovered of late, a budding artist. Instead she was one of a gazillion under-appreciated moms of her generation.

Who knows how it was to be inside the skin of their day-to-day lives, but from this vantage point, now they appear to be reaping the joys of all their hard work. I sigh with envy. Their life, and their relationship, is now one big vacation–or so it seems. Sure, they still have laundry to do and bills to pay (at least my mom does), but they go on nice vacations, they winter in Florida, play lots of golf, go to yoga (my dad likes to work on his core), get to spend as much time together as they please, and are still married and affectionate with each other after forty-five years. I sure can't wait for the day that Brad and I get there . . . on some days, though, I'm afraid we might die trying.

Despite the award-winning example set by my mother, she had to tackle only two roles: Wife and Mother. At first, I thought I could handle it. I even tried to be a superhero: *Wife! Mother! Star Employee!*

I aspired to *Have It All.* Like most of my girlfriends, I believed that I could deliver on every goal and fulfill every need, on time, to every single person who needed something from me. After all, we were fabulously successful, twenty-first-century-type gals.

I remember exactly when I realized "Having It All" was really just "The Big Lie." I had just recently returned to work after my maternity leave following the birth of my second child. I was racing home to meet the nanny. I was running late because I had misplaced my keys and I had to walk from the parking garage all the way back to my office, search my desk, the bathroom, the lobby and the elevator, and for kicks, our attractive male receptionist (just kidding). I was hiking back to the parking garage with my cell phone, and Brad on the line.

"Hey! Where are you? I need you to bring me a key to the Blazer."

"Why, where are your keys?" he asked.

"How the heck do I know? I have turned this sixty-story office tower on its head and I cannot for the life of me find my blasted keys. I'm going to be late meeting the nanny and she's going to dock me like twenty-five bucks a minute if I'm late."

The whole time I was talking to him, I was huffing through the atrium of said sixty-story, state-of-the-art office tower for the third time to my car. It is about an eleven-minute walk door-to-door. I had now done this *three times.*

"Maybe they dropped near my car?" I reasoned, trying desperately to think what I could have done with those stupid keys. "I'll call you when I get to the car and let you know for sure."

The keys were, in fact, there, but not under the car. What I had missed my other three trips to the car was that they were *in the ignition.* I had left them there that morning, as I came screeching into the garage on two wheels, already late for some inane meeting for which I was woefully unprepared because my oldest had been up all night with some weirdo cough that sounded like fingernails on the proverbial chalkboard. And while I was convinced my daughter would die that very night, she was fine and I alas was holding my eyelids open with pickup sticks the next day.

So not only were the keys in the ignition . . . but the car had been parked and *running all day long!* How was it possible that my car was still there and had enough gas to run all day? And why hadn't I noticed the fact that the car was running when I got out of the car, and returned to it twice looking for the keys?

That was when reality screamingly collided with fantasy.

I realized that I could not now, nor ever, have it all. I was shocked and embarrassed that I couldn't pull it off. But then I realized that it is virtually impossible for *anybody* to pull off–no matter how well educated, organized, prepared, and enthusiastic (when all else failed, I tried to play the enthusiasm card, but thinly veiled enthusiasm doesn't mask sheer contempt, I've found). Most women my age had been schooled that if you attend a good college, work hard, coordinate the right internships, and put in the hours, you will be rewarded with a good career, above-average pay, and opportunity for advancement. No one ever coached me on what to do when career and home are at such cross-purposes that you don't know whether you are coming or going. What do you do when you want it all–to be with your sweet baby and to continue on this career track for which you sacrificed so much before you got married and had said baby? Did I have to sacrifice one baby for another?

My boss was the poster mom for working women. Donning

her short bob, Brooks Brothers suits, and seriously professional demeanor, she nearly resembled a man, which was the idea back in the early nineties, wasn't it? Logging sixty-hour weeks and juggling two kids and a husband, I was regaled with stories about how she put her kids to bed in their school clothes to cut down on prep time the next morning, or how she fed her kids frozen waffles on a stick in the car on the way to preschool. Before I had kids, I was mildly amused by her ingenuity. After I had kids, I was appalled. Surely, *I* could do better.

But it turned out that as much as I hustled, planned, crashed, juggled, hoped, dreamed, and gritted my teeth, I could not do better . . . and be happy and sane and good at anything. I was shocked. I was a polite feminist and wasn't this what the movement was all about–equal pay, equal opportunity, and most important, the guilt-free pleasure to pursue a career without judgment? I deserved and was entitled to the success that I had worked so hard and so long for. I was a vice president and officer in the company. There was a lot of blood, sweat, and tears invested in that business card I handed out at meetings. Not to work was unthinkable to me and certainly unthinkable to my husband, who was equally proud of my career achievements. And just as important, me not working was unthinkable to our budget. But at the same time, walking out the door every morning and leaving my Mary Poppins of a nanny to delight in my sweet babies every day . . . well, that was unthinkable, too.

There were no training books or seminars for this. Believe me: I checked. My own wonderful mom was of no help either.

Back in the sixties, she had quit her job when my brother and I were born, and that was the end of her brief foray in the working world. I know that there are plenty of moms, married and single, who don't have the luxury of a Mary Poppins, and drop off their kids at some marginal day care every day because that is what circumstances demand. I realized that I sounded bratty and immature as I whined and fretted over my dilemma, especially to my friends who had to work no matter how bad it got. And I'm sure I annoyed those who had decided to stay home (and of whom I was secretly, or not so secretly, jealous). On occasion, I was outright mean to them.

I hadn't prepared myself for this challenge and mourned the loss of this dream of having it all. I bitterly fought against the fact that there was a big lie. I felt betrayed and angry and confused and tired. In fact, I had never been more tired. This revelation was a shock to the system and it took me a few weeks and lots of wine to absorb it. And while I was especially sensitive to those who passed judgment on my decision to work, no one judged me more than myself.

Motherhood is a tricky business. And like all jobs, we each bring different skill sets to the table. So there are women out there who are better moms because they work. And there are moms who want to be at home, should be at home, and absolutely bask in the glow of all things maternal and sweet. And then there are the rest of us–struggling for the right answers, because what seems like the right answer one day only stands you on your head the next. And in the meantime, all these child-rearing experts are fighting over whether kids suffer in day care, suffer in the arms of a nanny, or suffer at home with a lazy mom.

And in some ways, that's what is underneath all this infighting among us girls. It's hard to own up to such a major confession–that despite us all wanting the same thing, we all want it in a different way. And since none of us really knows what we're doing in the beginning anyway, we plagiarize each other or our mothers or our grandmothers–that's human survival. We learn by doing and by watching others and by copying them. And no one, at least no one I know, likes to think they're making the wrong decision. So in order for me to be right, you have to be wrong . . . right?

But the bottom line for me was–did my kids suffer when I worked full-time? Absolutely not. But I will tell you what: *I* did. I suffered through work meetings wondering what Mary Poppins was feeding my baby for lunch. I avoided business travel as much as I could (certain that I would die in a fiery accident and Brad would have to explain to our daughter that Mom "chose" work over her). When I did have to travel, I resented every minute I was out of town, sure that my child would forget the sound of my voice. Client issues seemed so ridiculously banal that I had no tolerance for them. So at the end of a long, painfully exhausting day, soon after the incident of the running car in the garage, I decided to try a new approach. I ceded that I could not have it all, but that maybe, just maybe, with some careful planning and a lot of faith, *I could have a bit more of what I wanted.*

Next came the hard work–figuring out what I wanted and

how much I was willing to do and willing to sacrifice to get it. When I could answer that question, perhaps I could better master my destiny, and isn't that what we all want? So I sat down with Brad, and we hammered out a strategy where I would cut back on my hours (and pay). We took a financial hit for the sake of everybody's happiness (okay, mostly mine, but ever hear of the trickle-down theory?), and decided to forgo some necessities and luxuries that my full-time salary provided. I felt like a saner employee and a better mother. Was I a better wife? I'm not sure it even crossed my mind.

Since this personal and professional epiphany, I am now on a mission to tell the younger women in my office about the Big Lie. I am encouraging them to think about what they want their lives to look like before they get married or have kids. I advise them not to settle for what they think they deserve or what they think they should do, but what they really want. In fact, I think there is a whole new business seminar category out there–"The Big Lie: How to Merge the Professional and the Personal with Grace and Style." And I'll tell you what else, I'll be telling my daughter and the daughters of my friends the same story. I certainly don't have all the answers and that's really the point, isn't it? No one does. There is no textbook scenario for this–after all, my idea of balance might not be the same as yours. But I do know this . . . A successful career? A functional family? A happy husband? Pick two, I will tell them. And we'll work from there. After all, isn't there a season for everything?

At first, I picked a functional family and a successful career . . . that wasn't working out that well, as you know, with me leaving cars running all day in the parking garage and all. Then I realized that to make my life work, my marriage had to work first, and that required from me even more work. So in a seismic shift, I aspired to have a happy husband and a functional family. Work, while it's still very important to me, for now has taken a backseat. Currently, managing life outside the office is rarely Brad's responsibility. Brad loves our children and our family and is quite helpful (although not handy) around the house. But he really never has to worry about managing the nanny, signing permission slips, or staying home when a child has to miss school. And if I'm scheduled to be in Rochester for a giant new-client meeting? Well, I'm the one calling a mother-in-law, a neighbor, or a best friend to make it work. In some ways, I was okay with that lopsided distribution of work. It helped me assuage my guilt as a working mom. And the hours I spent *at work* signing up for soccer, coordinating ballet carpool, and managing school paperwork? Well, my boss would be appalled and my husband would never do it.

One of the most brutal parts of getting out of the fast lane at work, and taking a part-time role, was that I had to check my ego at the door. It was tough. After a career spent working my way to a killer corner office, I had to hire and train my replacement, and move into a position, and office, more suitable for a part-timer. I was no longer invited to high-level meetings . . . they were often late in the day or on days I wasn't in the office. I was no longer the go-to person for a team of young executives that I had hired, trained, and mentored. I thought it would be so easy to give up control, give up a window office, give up a team of bright people, give up the fast track. After all, I was giving up all this power and control for a really good thing . . . the slow track. But dang, sometimes it really stank. Because working was something I knew how to do. Being at home, even part of the time? Well, that was new territory.

Now I am in the trenches of family life, managing the minutiae of daily life–dishes, laundry, groceries, cleaning, cooking, putting stuff away, matching socks, sorting paperwork. Alternate that with putting on my Career Girl hat at the office and some days I feel positively dizzy about who I am supposed to be. While this is what I wanted, the details of running a family and working don't always play to the strengths of Big Picture Girl. On occasion, this has resulted in me having a standoff with things like my dishwasher, to see if I could possibly go another day without unloading it. Yes, I know my dishwasher is an inanimate object, but sometimes I swear it's laughing at me as I bend over to unload it for the umpteenth day in a row.

So it's a good thing that Brad has been pretty supportive. He's good about not bringing work home with him and helping out when he's home in the evenings. Since he's employed by the World's Greatest Company, he has a remarkable–and probably unusual–work/life balance. Up until five years ago, Brad worked with me at an ad agency. But what Brad saw in his new company was not only a great career advance for him, but a wonderful attitude that would allow him to participate in family life: They actually believe that wonderful old cliché–people work to live, not live to work. Brad heads out early–he's at his desk typically by 7:30 A.M.–and he does travel more. But when he's in town, he's usually home by 6. He can take over with homework time, help with dinner, and get the kids bathed and in bed. Getting that help from him made it possible for me to have the energy to deliver on The Gift.

Back in 2003, when I was working toward balance, Brad and I felt that we were losing out on achieving any sort of balance of responsibilities, and worse, battling through a never-ending power struggle. Flying home from California, where Brad had invited me along on a business trip, we were rehashing again some tired point about who was supposed to do what. There was nothing like sitting on a five-hour flight home stuffed in coach to get the bickering started: "If I have to remember and track every birthday in *your* family so that I can remind *you* to send a birthday card and gift, then why don't I just send the darn gift myself?" I asked.

"I told you I would take it off your plate–it's my family, I'll do it."

"Well, if I have to tee you up every time, you're not really doing it, are you?" Back and forth, back and forth. Good times.

We were turning our airline-induced indigestion into major-league ulcers as we haggled about whose responsibility buying stupid birthday gifts for his family was. It was definitely a sore point between us, as we had gotten in trouble before about late gifts, delinquent birthday wishes, and the lot. And then I had a brilliant–and I mean blindingly brilliant–idea: Muller Family job descriptions. Yes, friends, I have added to my résumé being

COO of the Muller House, while Brad is the CEO. We trade CFO responsibilities back and forth, but they've landed in Brad's court the last several years–which doesn't speak necessarily to his strong financial acumen, as he is only barely more competent than I, and I'm an utter money loser (figuratively and literally).

Stay-at-home mommyhood isn't a given once babies arrive, and husbands aren't always the main breadwinners. Nowadays you're supposed to be in a marriage of equals–splitting responsibilities. However, does everything really have to be equal? What if Brad and I decided to play to the strengths of each partner? No more tit for tat, no more: "I did this so now it's your turn to step up" and on and on and *on.* Instead, you get a say on those issues in which you have a vested interest, firsthand knowledge, or some sort of expertise. Case in point: Brad has no say in a new washing machine, except for how much it costs as he has an interest in our budget. But since he has no firsthand knowledge of how a washing machine works, nor any expertise in doing laundry, I get the final decision.

The job descriptions have served as a nice set of guardrails over the years–we don't have to nag each other about stuff and endure all that back-and-forth about "have you done this?" or "have you done that?" There are five key categories of our responsibilities–children, house/family, finances, spouse, and social, plus a general overview. These roles are not a tool to lord over the other in a prickly and picky kind of way. I know what you want to ask, and no, there is no category for intimacy. We made this plan three years ago, for goodness' sake–I wasn't the highly evolved and acutely tuned-in spouse that I am today! Sadly, it still never occurred to me that I was not focused on being a better wife to whasisname, you know that tall guy with the nice green eyes? That came later.

Reflecting back on this time when I was juggling everything and still dropping the ball on intimacy, I decided to ask Brad about it. He said that he didn't think he was being neglected on the days that he wasn't aiming for sex and it wasn't on my radar. He was raised by a single mom who worked full time, his dad was never around after the divorce, and they struggled financially to make ends meet.

"Since I didn't have the experience of being raised in a two-parent family, no one modeled affectionate spousal behavior for me. When I got married, it was all gravy. I was thrilled to be with you, and glad I was no longer a bachelor who had to fend for himself in the kitchen. Life had never been better for me. After the kids, the trade-off of little or no sex seemed like a sacrifice, but I was willing to make it in order to keep my wife happy (and sane) and to maintain the semblance of the good life I had come to know and enjoy. I had a great job, a healthy boy and girl, a fine home, and good friends and neighbors. The lack of sex that we had could be ignored. After all–there is a price to pay for everything."

Ouch.

While Brad wasn't ready to throw out the baby with the bathwater, there was an undercurrent of tension, but I was too darned busy to notice it. It would be an interesting experiment if, in relationships, we could get recognized for a job well done.

Because when you're used to the highly structured world of work and reward, a lack of immediate payoff is a challenging transition. There are no promotions, no 360-degree reviews from your peers, no nice lunches or celebrations when you close the big deal or win the big account. And no one popping by your office to say, "You were on fire in that meeting! Great work!" I'm not even going to talk about motherhood as the most thankless job of all, as Hallmark and my grandmother have covered that sentiment quite well over the years, thanks.

But if we took some lessons from the business world and applied them to marriage, I think we'd all agree we're undervaluing our most important asset. And when it comes to intimacy, we're probably underutilizing a critical benefit. So along with specific job descriptions, Brad and I could be on a bonus structure based on performance. In the career world people get raises, promotions, luncheons, and cheesy plaques and/or desk ornaments. If we had a bonus structure attached to our spousal job descriptions, now that would be quite a game changer, wouldn't it? I mean, if someone told Brad that he would get paid $100,000 (just to name a number) to be the best husband and spouse for a year, according to a job description determined by *moi*, I'll bet he (and every other red-blooded husband out there) would jump on it like white on rice. I would, too–Hawaii, anyone?

Putting a lot of stuff, including intimacy, out on the kitchen table for discussion and negotiation should be an evolving process in a relationship–one that is moving through family issues, changing jobs, and increasing responsibilities. Working at an office that teaches you all about office politics is a good primer for trying out some of these principles at home. Reward, praise, but don't forget to try to fix things that are broken. And when all else fails, try a PowerPoint presentation.

My good friend Teresa is negotiating through issues of power and control in her marriage. Apparently her current mode of communication wasn't working as John told her one night, "I'm just so tired of living in Nagland." To which she nearly retorted, "Yeah, I know that place, it's across the river from 'You Suck-ville.' " But instead, she decided to try out some other tactics–not asking for help, not expecting help, and eventually not getting help. But that's a whole other chapter, isn't it? What really got me was how Teresa overcame the communications impasse–via PowerPoint. She developed a PowerPoint presentation entitled "How Teresa and John Can Get on the Same Page." "I drove over to his office one day and presented it to him," she said. How'd it go? "Well, I got through the presentation and then we started talking, so that's a good thing."

Whether I've been at home avoiding the dishwasher, or at the office all day putting some fade in a PowerPoint presentation, I can't wait to go out with my girlfriends. Every working woman, whatever her life's situation–married, unmarried, mother or not–deserves a night out. That's why my Book Club of nearly fifteen years is sacred territory. Unlike other groups of the same name, we actually do read and discuss the book of the month. We also drink wine, dish, and hang out together. We've been through marriages, divorces, babies, jobs, and other assorted life changes with each other. A lot of women have this outlet, whether it's a bunco group, a dinner club, or a craft guild (I have to admit I don't know anyone who belongs to a crafting organization, however). But the net result is the same: a safe place to communicate about issues that drive us nuts when we're at home.

After about a hundred days into my special year with Brad, I decided to let my hair down and fill my girlfriends, some of whom I've known since college, in on things. Besides, my experiment was kind of new and exciting. Boy, did that go over like a lead balloon.

"What were you thinking?"

"You're not really going to do it the whole *year*, are you?"

"Whatever you do, do *not* tell my husband."

"What will you do on special occasions?"

"Do you even like it? Having sex every day I mean?"

"Geez, I wonder if I could do it . . . for a week maybe."

"Girl, were you *drunk*?"

And that is just a little pu pu platter of responses.

But overall, I was pleasantly surprised by some–if not all–of my support. In fact, one night as I excused myself from "Girls' Martini Night" at a neighborhood bar, I got a few winks, nods, and even a "You go, girl!" After the initial shock wore off, there didn't seem to be much judgment. If there was, I wasn't aware of it. After getting over the amazement of my birthday tale and the requisite jokes, the girls recognized I was putting forth an earnest effort, and to that end, my friends were offering toasts of support. In a world where we're bombarded with petty jealousies and mean-spirited gossip, where women get pitted against each other on so many things, it was a nice feeling. It could have been that my gal pals were just grateful it was me and not them, and kept their snarky comments to themselves. But in reality, I think it was because I was taking a shot at an admirable goal and they were secretly rooting for me. I don't think any of them aspired to be me, mind you, but I do think we all, in our nutty, overscheduled lives, aspire to have a better, closer connection with our spouse. And they thought I might be on to something.

And after only a few months, I *knew* I was on to something. I was grateful for my small cadre of supporters. Perhaps it doesn't matter if you work or stay at home, send your kids to private or public school, or belong to the country club or the YMCA, intimacy is a common experience–and apparently, a frequent dilemma–for all of us. Sometimes the things that are the most intensely personal are the things that happen to us all–or at least a lot of us. Like negotiating sex with your spouse. Intimacy is the great equalizer . . . whether we're rich or poor, black or white, educated or not, city dweller or farm girl, intimacy is the glue that binds a relationship together.

In contrast, Brad told *no one.* Not even his best friend. I was surprised.

"You told me that most husbands in America would be thrilled with this gift, so why aren't you telling anyone?"

"Well," he said, "first of all, it's our business. And second, it's not like it's a normal part of the conversation for me."

Oh, *riiiggght.* I forgot. Women talk about the intricacies of their lives all the time–husbands, kids, sex, neighbors. And men talk about . . . heck, I must not know the first thing about what guys talk about because I thought they talked about *sex*!

NOVEMBER

Blessed Be the Ties That Strangle . . . I Mean Bind

"Hey, hon, you-know-who called," Brad said as I walked in the door with a cooler to brine our fourteen-pound turkey for Thanksgiving.

I heaved the cooler up on the counter. "Oh, yeah? What did you say? Did you do my dirty work for me and tell her that I couldn't volunteer on her committee?" I asked.

"No, I told her you were out for the day–singlehandedly building a Habitat House with only hand tools–and blindfolded."

"Nice! Did she get the hint?"

"Of course not, she wants you to call her right away. Before you do, let's practice together. Look at me. Just say no. Say it with me–NOOOOOOOO." He did this while squeezing my cheeks to form an O shape. I tried, but my lips simply wouldn't form the words.

"That's ridiculous," Brad said. "You never had trouble telling me *no."*

* * *

Well, he had that one right.

Why is it that I, and many women I know, can't say no to the PTA, church, children's theater, neighborhood association, or soccer club, but we can say no to our husbands day in and day out? My girlfriend says she wakes up each morning and has to decide who she's going to be today–PTA Mom, Carpooler, Designer and Small Business Owner, Laundress/Maid, Cook, and so on. "I never wake up and decide, 'Today is the day I'm going to be a Wife.'" In the era of Wives Who Do It All, many of us are not doing "It" at all. Instead, we're overextending ourselves with work, school, church, synagogue, garden club, and so on.

But here's the truth, at least for me: Everyone knows when you're *not* volunteering at school, driving your kids to choir, or getting a covered dish to the neighborhood picnic. You're either doing it or you're not. But no one knows if you're *not* having sex with your spouse (except for your spouse, of course). You can be the most admired person on the block for spreading good deeds and goodwill from one end of town to the other, but few husbands are going to ask for volunteer help to get their wives back in the mood and back in the bedroom. Can you imagine the e-mail? "Hey, everyone, we're looking for one or two folks who can spare a few hours for a great cause–Phil needs some help or suggestions on how to get Jennifer in the intimacy groove. If you have experience falling off the intimacy horse and can help, e-mail me today! Thanks and have a great day."

For a long time I put things that were important, but never the most important, ahead of my relationship with my husband. Serving as chair of the board of the weekday school. Teaching Sunday school. Planning neighborhood socials. Drafting the newsletter for the elementary school. Juggling client demands. Staffing conference calls from home while fixing dinner and folding laundry. Calling my mother . . . my best friend . . . my sister-in-law . . . my old babysitter to check in. Hitting the "refresh" button on my e-mail about, oh, 258 a times day. Baking cookies for . . . (well, nothing really, I just like to bake cookies). Certainly these things are not unimportant–in fact, I consider cookie baking to be very important! But so is Brad. While I would have told any telemarketer who called to poll me about my marriage that on a scale from 1 to 5, with 5 being *very important*, my marriage was, indeed, a 5, I wasn't living that affirmation out day to day.

I realized that the bustle of my daily life was fraught with missed opportunities to connect with my spouse, and when I layered on the added chaos of the holidays, getting up close and personal was even more of a challenge. So in this season of Thanksgiving I realized that I needed to slow down and reorder some things. While I was thankful for school, church, my neighborhood, and so on, what I needed to be most thankful for was all that resided inside the four walls where I lived–my children, my husband, and the gift of intimacy, which has been a gift to us both, really.

I decided to try my best to say yes to all that this holiday represents and to actually enjoy this time of Thanksgiving–

leisurely time spent with family . . . and with Brad. I would relax, kick back, and focus on those quality activities that used to bring me so much pleasure. Yes, the national pastimes of the Thanksgiving season–watching television, grossly overeating, and napping.

I recently met a woman who doesn't have a television and I wondered how on earth she would be spending her Thanksgiving. No Macy's Thanksgiving Day Parade? No football? No *Sound of Music*? She is not some weird freak lady (at least I don't think she is, but we did just meet). She's nice, attractive, and married with children. I mean, she *seems* normal. She joked about how much she doesn't know since she doesn't watch television and I thought, "Dang straight, how do you get through the day?" But then I reconsidered all the absolutely ridiculous, bottom-of-the-barrel television drivel that won't taint her brain and take up her leisure time, which does taint and take up mine.

A few years ago, I was addicted to two kinds of television. The first was bad television, and I mean really, really *bad* television that had absolutely no redeeming social value. The kind of television programming that when it was over made me feel slightly queasy. You know how your mother used to tell you, "If you get that funny feeling inside when you're doing something, it probably means you shouldn't"? Well, that's how I felt when I watched that kind of television. I knew I shouldn't be watching it. I didn't even laugh or learn anything, save for how depraved television is these days. This is not art or high-concept television–it's low-brow television programming that neither my children nor your children should ever, ever see. Mostly they were reality shows about washed-up celebrities, washed-up relationships, weight and self-image issues, surviving in the Everglades with only a paper clip, raising dysfunctional families, or people simply acting like fools because a camera was pointed at them. In fact, half the time I was sitting there watching it thinking to myself, "I can't believe that this trash is on regular cable! I mean, really!"

I loathed myself when it was over because I could not ever get that time back. It was lost forever into that diminishing black hole called Charla's Brain. What kind of great artwork could I have created during that time? Could I have taken up a musical instrument, or finally read *War and Peace*, or learned more about climate change, or invested wisely in the stock market? Really, I understand why Jane Austen was able to write all those great books–no TV! But I rationalized that I needed my downtime, those moments when I could take off my Supermom cape and hunker down into some mindless television. And after some seriously tedious numbing, I realized that I needed to go to sleep, but my head was spinning and I was overdosed on what not to wear, how not to walk down the runway, or how not to get picked for a date. Sadly, it did not occur to me that I was trading an opportunity to hunker down with Brad.

Then this sensory overload came to a head and I had to stop the madness! I was not getting to the important things: reading books and magazines, doing my homework for my Bible study, sifting through my favorite cookbooks, scanning the paper. I realized I really had to exercise some discipline and curb my television time–it was taking up valuable time, if not a wee bit of energy flipping around to all those channels. And it wasn't like I was bonding with Brad over some weepy Hallmark movie or discussing Tim Russert's guests. I had gotten lazy and complacent with my evenings and it needed to end. And so I went on a bad television strike. While I did cross the picket line once or twice (hey, a girl's gotta have a little *American Idol*, right?), I was feeling less disgusted with myself, and found that I was more sociable. The only drawback I worried about was that this might compromise my ability to dish pop culture with friends. But then I discovered a little secret: You don't have to *watch* television to know what's happening *on* television. Guys, by the way, have known this for years–hence the advent of *Sports Illustrated* and *ESPN The Magazine*. You can read who just got voted off an island/out of the house/out of the kitchen/etc. on the Internet. You can pick up *People* magazine to read about the latest plot of the hot network shows.

My girlfriends didn't believe me when I announced I had gone on a televisions strike as I could still chitchat about it with authority. "Don't hand me that line about not watching television!" they would exclaim. Peruse any tabloid magazine in the grocery store line, friends, and you, too, can be an expert on bad television without actually watching bad television. I kid you not. I realize that I have transferred my problem instead of really solving it, but it works for me. Now, I'm spending time with Brad, reading more, and sleeping better than I ever have before.

The second kind of television is happily enthralling programming that I do advocate–and still watch–cooking shows. They are a tiny little sweet spot in my day. Cooking shows are the antithesis of junky television. I adore them, I relish them (ha), I bask in them. Cooking shows make me glad, sometimes very nearly giddy. And they occasionally make me laugh. Cooking shows are like *Leave It to Beaver*: Everyone is happy and cheery (granted, some are ingratiatingly happy and cheery) as they prepare gorgeous food in well-lit, beautifully decorated kitchens. Everything they need is at their fingertips–*they are never without* (again the opposite of reality shows where everyone seems to be in want of something–money, love, peace, fame, a new living room, or beauty). Somebody has bought all the food, probably without two grumpy and hungry children in tow, pre-prepped the herbs and vegetables, and within minutes they are creating sustenance with grace and ease.

These cooks and chefs are showcasing their talents instead of revealing their deepest darkest flaws and secrets (and we're all better off, don't you think). The impressive knife skills when chopping an onion, the quick flick of the wrist when handling a crepe, or the ability to pinch the perfect piecrust. I DVR my cooking shows and watch them often–my kids watch them with me and they know by name the hosts of my favorites. It's one of the few things on TV that we can watch together and everybody is happy. Because on cooking shows, everybody wins. And unlike bad television, cooking shows are inspirational–I, too, will be serenely happy once I can roast a side of lamb on an open pit for twenty of my closest friends. I feel like I am a better person having watched them . . . well, at least a little.

But in November I get less time with my cooking shows, because the Sports Mafia has shanghaied my television, my house, and my marriage. Not to mention, I'm cooking like a fool anyway. To my dismay, the DVR (and I love you, DVR, but please, I need more from you!) can tape only two shows at the same time, or else Brad would be taping golf, NFL, *and* baseball. The real problem here is there aren't sports *seasons* anymore. Nearly all professional sports run year-round. Baseball is not just in the summer, and the NHL is not just in the winter. Heck, the World Series is in November! And ice hockey is in June? Golf is year-round and the NBA? Don't get me started on that freak show. So Brad's living vicariously through his sports teams, and I'm busy aspiring to be the next Ina Garten, and we meet in the middle, at our kitchen table.

As a result of less television and more intimacy, I was sleeping better, feeling better, and watching my happy cooking shows at my leisure on my DVR. I couldn't believe my good fortune: It was as if I had discovered the Holy Grail. Intimacy Every Day – Junky Television + My Favorite Foodies on DVR = Better Sleep and a Happy Spouse. Hurray for me!

Thanksgiving is really a fantastic holiday for us: me as a food lover and Brad the sports fan. I love to entertain. I love it, love it, *love* it. (Luckily Brad does, too, or does now after ten years of being with me.) The cooking component didn't always come easy to me, but at least I don't have to go overboard on decorating my house (see December)–some happy mums for my porch, and turkey dinner napkins, and I'm done. I can focus on researching menus, preparing meals, setting a gorgeous table with the wedding china, and enjoy hanging out with family. Except, of course, when we have to watch sports. The tradition of Detroit and Dallas hosting NFL tilts on Thanksgiving is nearly as old as the holiday itself, according to Brad, who also had to explain to me the meaning of a tilt (which is code for a "really, really exciting game"). His grandmother was the biggest football fan in his family, and when she hosted his Thanksgivings in years past, she would time serving fourteen people turkey and all the fixin's between games so as not to miss a snap.

But before I lugged out my roasting pans, I had an important commitment I simply couldn't miss: my son's last Thanksgiving feast at his preschool. This time next year, my little fellow would be walking the halls of elementary school, riding the bus, and learning to read. If I could only stop time and savor longer this enchanted day, when my boy and his tiny friends were dressed in handmade brown paper bag costumes with paper hats and feathered headbands. Some were Indians and some were Pilgrims, and they were feasting on *authentic* First Feast fare: chicken nuggets, cornbread, and mac and cheese. I was caught up in a moment so pure and engaging that it nearly overwhelmed me. Children this age are so very kind and generous, and they reminded me that Thanksgiving is about being thankful, of course, but it's also about being kind and generous.

So I went from being feted by five-year-olds in the church gymnasium to trying to be as generous and kind in hosting Brad's family, which includes his mom, sister, brother, brother's wife, and their two kids. Six adults and four kids. I had a Wednesday evening dinner, brunch, and Thanksgiving menu on Thursday and a plan for Friday and Saturday. Easy peasy. I planned out my menu (and not around kickoff). I had made list after list, and sketched out my week and what I would prepare on Tuesday, Wednesday, and finally, Turkey Day. I shopped the Farmer's Market, the Fresh Market, and the local supermarket. My grandmother's cheese ball (which is like a proper noun–my daughter asks: "Are you making Cheese Ball?") and marinated shrimp as appetizers. Then an oven-roasted turkey, which had been brined overnight in a concoction of honey and water; garlic mashed potatoes with gravy; sausage-pumpkin cornbread stuffing; roasted asparagus; and for dessert–pumpkin cheesecake with gingersnap crust for the adults, and Ooey Gooey Pumpkin Bars for the kids.

I also whipped some snacks together and breakfast items: a blue cheese and walnut spread, sour cream coffee cake with pears, and some homemade chocolate chip oatmeal cookies. I also had waiting in the wings a new recipe for turkey soup. (Brad loves turkey soup after Thanksgiving . . . or is it his mother?) Either way, my recipe included fresh spinach and cheese tortellini. And last but not least, made-to-order waffles from my awesome waffle iron like the ones they have at the Hampton Inn breakfast-included breakfast bar.

No stone was left unturned . . . no pantry cabinet left unstocked. I was *on it.*

But when Brad and I first got married, I had not yet mastered the art of putting forth a meal for so many all by myself.

For two reasons, really. One, I wasn't that adept in the kitchen. Yes, it's true–there are a few people from the South who don't ever learn how to cook. Two, I never had the need to cook anything–much less all by myself. In hindsight, spending every major holiday previous to getting married at my grandmother's house with three generations of cooks was a real culinary deficit for me–there was no room, no need, and certainly no opportunity for me to cook. My grandmother, mother, two aunts, and a few older cousins were clucking around that teensy kitchen like a bunch of mother hens tending to casseroles, meats, vegetables, biscuits and breads, and a dizzying array of desserts. Family members were flowing in the screen door with insulated casserole carriers holding even more food. I had not eaten a Thanksgiving meal prepared by someone who didn't have the name *Snow* somewhere in their family history until I was thirty years old. (Except for the time my college roommate got married over Thanksgiving weekend and I ate with her family . . . including her great-aunt Zelda, with whom I also shared a room that entire weekend. Again, I just showed up for the meal . . . and helped Aunt Zelda with her zipper a time or two.)

So in the early years of our marriage I wasn't used to the idea of sharing holidays with someone not related to me by blood and I certainly wasn't used to the idea of preparing a holiday meal for someone not related to me by blood. So in the early years of our marriage, the planning and execution of a meal simply overwhelmed me. Not to mention having to clean and generally hose down the house before and after the event. And while Brad was handy with a vacuum, he brought nada cooking skills to our beautiful union. In fact, I think the only thing he brought of culinary note might have been a George Foreman grill and a recipe for spaghetti sauce, which included ground beef, canned sauce, and an entire bottle of dried oregano. Yum. We never hosted my family–who were still heading over the river and through the woods.

In those early years when I was responsible for putting a turkey on the table for Brad's family, I managed to muddle through, including the year that I was pregnant with our son and was so skeeved out by that slimy beige bird that I had to lie down on the couch and shout directions to Brad and his sister on how to stuff the turkey. Back then the stress of it all did not lend itself to me wanting to celebrate the season with Brad between the sheets. I was so exhausted from entertaining his family that I certainly didn't have the energy or inclination to entertain anything else. If Brad was interested in something other than seconds of turkey and dressing, forget it. Catty, no? If it made some awkward moments between us, I didn't notice. But I was trying . . . at least in the kitchen. I had acquired an insulated casserole carrier and a deviled egg dish. I was trying new dishes and experimenting with recipes. Brad was happy at the thought of hosting his family (it was our year with his side), and I was learning about organization and prep work and menu planning.

So this year, no worries! Some years of practice, and not being pregnant, meant that I was preparing a delish Thanksgiving Feast *and* dishing up some daily intimacy with Brad. Now, I'm motoring around the kitchen each day and then each evening motoring down the hall for some good tidings of intimacy with Brad, and then right back into the kitchen to pack up my cooled cookies and check on my setting cheesecake. I was in my Nigella zone–sexy and culinary–no doubt about it.

And I stayed in the zone and on task until about 5 P.M. on Thanksgiving Day. Right after that beautiful meal (if I do brag so myself) was put forth in our dining room and enjoyed by six grateful adults and four messy children. I took the turkey out a bit early (my brother-in-law and I both *swore* that meat thermometer registered 180 degrees!) so after much fussing we had to put it back in the oven again. My asparagus was slightly overroasted, but the stuffing was outstanding and the potatoes were nearly pitch perfect (and quite garlicky). And the *pièce de résistance*–my homemade pumpkin cheesecake with gingersnap crust lovingly baked in a water bath. It was scrumptious, so scrumptious in fact that my dear sister-in-law turned to me and said, "This cheesecake is incredible . . . where did you buy it?" I about spewed cheesecake down my twin sweater set. I was so very, very sad that someone would think that *my* cheesecake, gently whipped with two pounds of cream cheese and so lovingly baked in a bath of steaming water, was *store-bought.* My sister-in-law came by this comment honestly. Her family thinks store-bought desserts are great–behold frozen éclairs and Mrs. Smith's pies. I put it down to misunderstandings between the North and South, and called the day a success.

Later, while folks ooh'ed and aah'ed over my culinary masterpieces and cleared the table, my feet started aching, my head started pounding, and I started to crash. I'd been running on

Thanksgiving adrenaline since Monday and I was just going to sit . . . down . . . for . . . one . . . little . . . minute . . . and . . . rest . . . my . . . feet . . . With that, I fell asleep on the couch in a roomful of people scurrying around my kitchen packing up food, washing dishes, soaking pans, and picking the meat off the turkey for the soup and stock . . . God bless my mother-in-law, who always picks the meat off the turkey for the soup and stock no matter whose house she is at for Thanksgiving.

Even with my high social needs and bizarre bursts of culinary energy, there are times when I simply need a break–even if the leftovers aren't cool yet and I'm snoring shamelessly in the middle of post-dinner chaos. Later, I would hop up and retire to my bedroom–one of the nice things about The Gift was that it could become a regular part of the "Rest and Relaxation Repertoire." Before, I would have snuck off to take a nap, or read a magazine–preferably alone. It was an opportunity for me to escape for a bit from Brad's family and from some really bad pinot grigio. I would head upstairs to model my Martyr Crown in front of the mirror–why, yes, it still fit perfectly after a day of cooking, cleaning, and slaving for my in-laws. It wasn't that I didn't like Brad's family and they certainly have never, ever insisted that I cook, clean, or slave for them. I was doing what I had seen my grandmother and mother and aunts and cousins do all those years–knock themselves out. Which was why I missed holidays with my family, where I could kick back, relax, and most certainly *not* knock myself out.

Now that I have committed to a new way to relax and renew, I can make eye contact with Brad (he knows the signals), and we can slip off for a "Doubles Nap." It's great–I get to have my husband to myself for a few minutes before I have to lend him back to his "first" family; we both get a breather from a giant meal and we can have a few moments of conversation about who said what to whom at dinner and if so-and-so was drunk or is he always that obnoxious. On occasion, however, I fall asleep on the couch along with the rest of the family who gorged out on turkey and stuffing. And that's okay, too.

The years we spent at my grandmother's house for Thanksgiving, there were too many people and not enough seats, so the luxury of falling asleep in a chair or on a sofa fell to the quick and the few. Some stretched out in front of the giant console (you read that right . . . a giant console) television to watch football. And fifteen minutes later they had joined in, too. It was not unusual for four to six people to be snoozing in that tiny den at any given moment after the Thanksgiving meal. Those of us who were awake didn't mind stepping around those who were asleep. "Does everyone just fall asleep like that?" Brad would ask. "Sure, it's the tryptophan, the extra helpings of biscuits, and the four kinds of *homemade* pie," I'd reply. "The real question is . . . how in the world do *you* stay awake?" I'd ask as I hunkered down in the corner with a pillow.

Certainly one of the glorious perks of a Thanksgiving meal is that divinely sated feeling. You are relaxed, a tad overfull, and those lovely turkey chemicals are making you feel nice and mellow . . . wow, an afterglow that feels eerily similar to sex! In a weird way, it is like a culinary dose of intimacy. Instead of sex, simply overeat on carbs and turkey–and *voilà*! But no, one of the gifts of getting older, after all, is getting wiser–wiser about how to cook a Thanksgiving dinner for twelve, wiser about how to balance work and family, wiser about *not* trying to do it all, and wiser about how best to connect with a spouse (and believe me, it's not overeating on turkey together). In the old days, the holidays were all about the status quo for me–not losing weight, for goodness' sake, but at least trying not to gain. Not always connecting with my spouse, but not completely ignoring him either. Not gaining much on my to-do list, but not losing too much ground either. This Thanksgiving, I was about more than damage control–I hadn't allowed anything to come between me and my special evenings with my husband and it was really, really good. Food? Well, I hadn't let anything come between me and a little cheesecake either. But one step at a time . . .

DECEMBER

The Ho Ho Ho Horribly Happy Holiday Season

"Well, honey, you ready for our daily deed?" I asked.

"I guess so—but it's pretty hard to feel frisky after watching Santa Claus Is Comin' to Town *for the umpteenth time and gorging on buttered popcorn," he said. "Can you give me a minute? I want to admire the tree for a little while and ponder Hermey's decision to be a dentist."*

And so it goes.

It's the most wonderful time of year again. A season of peace and goodwill toward man (I've found it much easier to feel goodwill toward mankind as a whole rather than goodwill toward the Christmas tree guy who gouged me on the price of a tree and some wimpy garland). A season high on sentimentalism and childhood memories. And a season where things are always just a little . . . bit . . . off.

When your normal to-do list is a mile long, it gets ten times longer during the working holidays. It gets hard to find time to do the regular stuff. You know, laundry, carpool, unloading the dishes, daily trysts. Sometimes I feel like I'm standing in the middle of a snow globe and someone is shaking it to kingdom come. But the biggest part of getting ready for the holidays definitely has to be getting the house just so.

My mother calls it fluffing. "Have you fluffed for the holidays?" she'll ask me. She wonders if I've decorated, and pulled out my boxes of ornaments, bows, and holiday figurines. I may sound like Scrooge, but I hate decorating my house for Christmas. I hate it, I dread it, and I utterly loathe it. I do want my house to look picture perfect for the holidays and I do want to create some more award-winning memories for my kids and family. But I hate the day we pull out fourteen tubs of Santas, ornaments, stockings, candles, placemats and napkins, books, and so on from the basement to start our fluffing. Because all I can think about is that day a few weeks later when I have to pack it up and put it away–or defluff, if you want to call it that. I hate the pine needles that have scattered everywhere. I abhor the leftovers oozing out of my fridge. I cry at the list of thank-you notes a mile long. Christmas is like a month-long dinner party–with guests that never leave and a hellacious mess. Merry merry.

Brad has made it easier, though, because he is a Christmas Tree Stud. I mean, if there were ever a contest for decorating a tree, he would win by a landslide–so just back away from the tree and no one will get hurt. For example, the man has some serious spatial skills, and searching for the perfect tree each season is much more successful because of him. Me? I'm wandering aimlessly through the maze of trees wondering which one is going to seep sap onto my hardwoods, all the while snapping pictures of the kids, hoping for a semidecent Christmas card photo. Brad is great at unrolling yards and yards of lights, each lovingly wrapped around a paper towel tube, and arranging them perfectly on the tree.

But most important, Brad has a happy heart for decorating a Christmas tree. And I do not. I have a happy and quite nostalgic heart *after* the tree is decorated and we sit on the couch and gaze lovingly at this festooned tree and proclaim, "Yep, this is the best one yet." But I don't really decorate the tree with a happy heart, and not even Christmas music and a hot toddy can help.

Weirdly enough, Brad came to our marriage with barely a stick of furniture, but with boxes and boxes of the most amazing tree accoutrements–garlands of stars, strings of red wooden balls that look like giant cranberries, sweet ornaments. Which is interesting because he nearly married someone who is not Christian. "You know," I once said, "this whole Christmas tree passion of yours might have been dead in the water if you had married someone who doesn't celebrate Christmas."

"Yeah, would that have been a buzzkill or what?" he replied as he stood on a ladder and carefully placed with great focus and concentration our homemade angel on the top of the tree.

I really do want a picture-perfect Norman Rockwell Christmas, just in my own dysfunctional way. And it's easy to forget that most family holiday memories are of the dysfunction, not the functional. Functional is not as memorable or compelling; it is not the stuff of family lore. More people remember the year that your uncle Bobby drank too much and mysteriously broke the toilet. That Christmas your cousin Billy came out of the closet. The season that your aunt Millie served raw meat and cold corn soufflé. As much as we try to create perfect holidays, holidays are really the perfect storm for drama.

I had never woken up at my own house on Christmas morning. It was always spent at my grandmother's house, my cousin's house, or my aunt and uncle's house. As a result, I had tremendous faith as a kid; if Santa could find me at a different address every year (which he always managed to do), then all must be right with the world. I discovered Santa's true identity later than my peers, primarily because I had seen him perform some amazing search-and-find feats. Who wants to give up on that?

My grandmother's dining room table was always chocablock crowded–too many chairs and not enough room for everybody. Even the sewing bench from the back bedroom and folding chairs from underneath the bed were pulled in to seat my parents, grandparents, and aunts and uncles. So another table was set in the front of the living room, near the front door. Bordering one side was a love seat that could accommodate two adults or three children, along with a wingback chair, a footstool, and other odd chairs, and that was where older cousins and spouses–about six to eight of us–sat. At the other end of the living room was a third table–a wobbly aluminum one that folded up and slid under a bed in the back bedroom. It, too, was covered with a tablecloth. That was the kids' table, and *that* was where I dined every Christmas Eve until I married. I never in all my life had a holiday meal at the "grown-up" table. Someone would have had to die to free up a space at the "grown-up" table, and there are three other cousins ahead of me anyway.

Grandmother's house was always jammed with bodies. To feed my extended family on Christmas Eve required a couple of sets of dishes and silverware, lots of paper cups and paper napkins, a cooler or giant Tupperware bowl of extra ice, and extra card tables to hold the food. We spread a tablecloth over my grandmother's washer and dryer to make more room for the food. Desserts were stored in the cool air outside, as there wasn't enough room in the fridge. We simply pulled them inside when the meal was over and people had enough room. Those holiday dinners were chaotic, loud, hot, and wonderful, and all I had ever known.

We played outside, running around in the yard, or stayed in, watching football or sitting around shooting the bull. There was much love and affection at those family gatherings. Close quarters in my grandmother's house dictated some of it, but we are also just a cheerful and engaged group.

Holidays with my family were a shock to my Midwestern-raised Brad. All that chaos and noise! "And do they always *hug* everyone like that, every time they see them? I don't really know their names yet–there are so many of them!" he once commented when we first visited. It could be a strain on your senses (and your personal space) if you weren't used to it. And since my grandmother did not permit drinking, he couldn't even take the edge off this claustrophobic lovefest with a nice cold beer or a glass of wine.

At my grandmother's, we would all stand in a circle weaving between tables and chairs and hold hands for a blessing, and my grandmother inevitably would break down in tears. "Well, Lord, I just thank you for all you have done for this family, and I'm just so thankful for our blessings because I know, Lord, well, Lord, this is probably my last Christmas. Amen."

She does this every year–announce to the world and to the Good Lord that this is her last. And all heck breaks loose and we all start talking at once to take turns fussing over her and telling her that, of course, this is not going to be her last Christmas, as she is healthy as a horse (and she is, or was) and that she very well may live forever, or at least as long as her sister Ima, who lived to be ninety-nine.

"Well, I am just so happy," she says with her voice trembling and her little white Aqua-Netted head bobbing up and down. "Because in all these years no one in this family has gotten divorced." My grandmother says this nearly every Christmas.

And she's right. With nearly thirty people in that room loading up plates with an appalling amount of food, none in our extended family are "dee-vorced," as my grandmother would say. My grandmother is so proud of this, but she is living proof that staying married does not always equate with being *happily* married. I sometimes think that very surely my grandmother would prefer you to be paralyzingly miserable beyond belief than dee-vorced. "Being unhappy isn't the worst problem in the world," she might have said. And that was what people of her generation truly believed.

And while they weren't dee-vorced, I can't tell you the last time my grandparents lived together; it must have been during the Nixon administration. They were married for thirty-five years, and after much sorrow and great upheaval, they settled into separate quarters. Never legally divorced, of course, but not really married, it seemed. I have no memory of my grandparents necessarily being affectionate with each other. Though I know that they continued to share meals, a garden, and somewhat of a life that spared them both what they most feared. Those were the times–divorce was unmentionable, unconscionable, and unbelievably not an option. So the family carved out a kind of truth that worked, but it was a tenuous arrangement up until my grandfather died.

My grandfather was warm with his grandchildren. And my grandmother, well, she was always getting food ready. We would spend Christmas Eve at my grandmother's house, where my grandfather would let himself quietly in through the sliding glass door after walking across her backyard from his house. He would leave the same way, with little fanfare. We knew where to find him if we needed him, which we did. My grandfather was irreverent, eccentric, complex, and on occasion loud. In some ways he was a man born in the wrong place and time, as some people are. In any other time, he would have been the charming, garrulous guest that you wanted to sit beside at a fantastic dinner party. In the rural foothills of North Carolina, he was a beloved father, brother, and son who brought his family tremendous love and occasional strife. My brother and I knew only the love and little of the strife and therefore revered him.

Legend has it (and old pictures prove it) that my grandfather was dark and broodingly handsome, and that my grandmother, who was smart and incredibly responsible, was smitten. My grandparents definitely broke Brad's Rule of Twos. She was older when they married, a ripe old twenty. She was a good student and my great-aunt Ima paid for her to attend secretarial school in Greensboro with the condition that if she married, she would repay the tuition. So Ima put up the money and my grandmother promptly repaid her not long after she got married–with delight, I've been told. My grandfather had nine siblings and my grandmother was the second youngest of sixteen children. For some unfathomable reason, my grandparents lived wedged in between both sets of in-laws and my grandmother cared for all four until they had all died. There were twenty-five sons and daughters who could have taken on the primary burden of caring for elderly parents, but somehow my grandmother bore the brunt of it all. Again, those were the times when nursing homes were unheard of and–like dee-vorce–not taking care of family was unmentionable, unconscionable, and unbelievably not an option.

Who knows if my grandparents had met today whether they would have gotten married. The world was smaller then–you met and married people in close geographic proximity to you. (That's why some people are so funny looking.) You met people in high school or in college or you married your best friend's cousin from out of town–which was always a big deal, especially if you lived in a small town that everyone was desperate to leave.

Marriage is now a choice, while back in the not-so-distant past, marriage might have been based on property, money, alliances, and other things unromantic; there was a time when women had little to no say in who their husband was going to be. The husband was chosen by one's family, father, village elder, etc. In fact, it's only been in the last several decades that women in industrialized societies have had the choice about whom they want to marry, and even if they want to marry. So being married to a spouse who didn't light your fire, well, that wasn't so strange back then. It was kind of like a game show gone bad . . . "And behind Curtain Number 2 . . . we have Earle! He's five feet five inches tall with a tractor, a twenty-acre plot of land, a domineering mother, and a small lean-to house with indoor plumbing. Earle's interests are priming tobacco, cleaning guns, going to church . . . and being able to feed himself and his mother until the next planting season. Let's give it up for Earle!" And I would think it fairly common back then that your husband might not trip your trigger in bed, since you didn't really pick him after all. So it was a doubly whammy–you were expected to be intimate with someone you probably didn't even choose. Fast forward to today–a lot of wives don't want to be intimate with the person they *did* choose. At least this is what I hear from girlfriends and on daytime television and often read in women's magazines. So now that we have the power to choose our own mates, things get all mucked up anyway.

My grandparents had a few family heirlooms to pass down to their children. There is a bedroom suite. There is my grandmother's high school class ring from 1936. There is an antique dish cabinet and some hand-quilted blankets. Some wonderful family photos. A few trinkets here and there that qualify as keepsakes only to our family, such as tiny hand-crocheted tree ornaments shaped like snowflakes, and a clay water pitcher with blue and red flowers. But families also pass down history–stories of bravery, hardship, and tragedy–as well as commonsense knowledge that helps sustain families: how to make butter and jam, how to birth a baby, when to plant things, when to put up the vegetables, how to make maxipads out of old sheets, how to build a barn, and so on. We'd like to think that these lessons and tales outlast our own short lives.

However, nobody in my big, loud, loving family passed down wisdom or commonsense advice about marriage, except to stay married no matter what the cost. No one discussed intimacy within the relationship. I am sure there are very few women, if any, in my age group who were counseled to marry someone with whom they are and would continue to be sexually compatible. For example, it would have been helpful to hear: "You know, darlin', you should really look for a guy who has the same sexual pace as you–it would really go a long way in smoothing out some of those longer-term issues about sex." But if they had, it means my girlfriends and I would have been shopping for a man who rarely, if ever, wanted to have sex after two kids and the age of forty. And how were we to know?

In fact, the triumvirate of marital woes (sex, money, and religion) isn't even acknowledged by most parents seeking to impart wisdom to their daughters. My family's advice did hit one out of three: "Marry a nice Christian boy and it will all work out." And what exactly does that mean anyway? I remember sitting down with Brad to talk about religion when we were newly engaged. Interestingly, it was Christmastime. A Baptist and an Episcopalian were coming together, and we could not be further apart on the Protestant continuum (but considering his first fiancée was Jewish, I didn't think we were that far apart). I mean, if you go to church–any church–it in some part signifies belief in God, right? So I asked him about it one night.

"Um, there's something we need to talk about," I said to Brad. "I mean, I know you believe in God, but I just need to hear that you really believe in God. Before we get married, I need to hear some statement of belief."

"Yeah, I believe," he responded.

I pushed. "What exactly do you believe?"

"What do you mean?" he asked. And he really meant it. This was before I knew that part of being Episcopalian for many was the grand vagueness of God–He could be different things to different people. And part of being Baptist, as many know, was the grand, unerring specificity of God.

So it turned out that we were more far apart than I thought. I was growing agitated. I mean, what's so hard about articulating what you believe? I blurted out, in my Baptist way, "Honey, I need to know if you believe that Jesus Christ is your Lord and personal Savior."

Huh? I had no idea where *that* came from. It was like in that exact moment I was channeling my grandmother, the one who doesn't believe in drinking or dee-vorce. I had alarmed him and surprised myself. And I don't blame him. I mean, if you aren't used to this kind of vernacular, it can sound strange. There I was, thinking I was marrying an "unbeliever," and he was thinking I was some kind of zealot. Apparently there was a wider gulf than expected–while Jesus should have been the common denominator among Christians, even Jesus is open to interpretation for Episcopalians. Brad did acknowledge he believed, at least in the abstract. Now it's all okay–we've bridged the gap and we're Methodist.

While I was surprised about negotiating religion in such a forthright way, I was expecting a certain amount of give-and-take when it came to merging his family and mine. Actually, I thought it would be a lot of take–me taking every opportunity to be with my family and not his. Which isn't fair, really. Brad has a perfectly nice family. But nobody can really appreciate the thinly veiled comment that you "marry the whole family" until you are married and you realize that you're now related to a whole new set of crackpots, and you don't find them nearly as interesting or tolerable as the bunch of crackpots that you are related to by blood. And at the very least, all the crackpots from *your* family like everything the same way you do. It's like when you're twelve, and you go to a sleepover at your best friend's house, and everything is different. The house smells strange, their habits are different, and they put onions in their scrambled eggs. And although you're having fun, you're so relieved to go back to your own familiar home and scrambled eggs with cheese.

When Brad first introduced me to my future mother-in-law, I thought it would be easy to win her over, but I was wrong. I would impart a wee bit of Southern charm, dotted with lot of polite "ma'ams" and exclamations of "You don't say!" But as we both started to dig a little deeper, I sensed this wasn't a sure thing. And this threw me off, because I generally do well on first impressions (it's those second and third impressions where it all goes downhill for me). So I found out that she likes to watch those ten-part series about the Civil War on PBS whereas I . . . well, I know who won the Civil War. She likes to read biographies on Thomas Jefferson and then discuss how Monticello was an intersection of architecture and horticulture unrivaled even today. Me? I only read fiction–preferably modern. She likes to *finish* the crossword puzzle *every day*. Me? I like Sudoku, the easy ones.

While she would never admit it and I can never be sure, I think she was a little unimpressed when she learned that I had gone to a public university. I mean, it's possible to see someone actually shudder, right? Despite the fact that UNC Chapel Hill is an outstanding and very competitive institution, and while there I attended one of the top five journalism programs in the country and later managed to get a job at a top public relations firm in New York City and actually pay my bills (well, most of them).

She attended a private college: Vassar. Her father, Yale. One brother is a doctor and the other a lawyer. Her sister also went to Vassar and works at Harvard, and she married a guy who heads up the graduate physics department there. I mean, these are some seriously freaky smart people. I was *way* out of my league and far away from my homespun Christmases at Grandma's house. But I will tell you that despite being so genetically gifted, many smart people have not a lick of common sense to even come out of the rain (present relatives who live in Boston and teach or work at Harvard excluded, of course).

I will tell you that while dining with the Harvard contingent one evening in Boston, and hearing about Brad's uncle's research into a fifth dimension (and no, this is not the coming of the age of Aquarius), I was the only one who knew what a Möbius strip was (present smarty pants who head up or work in the physics department at Harvard not included). So for one infinitesimal (that means tiny) moment, I felt a sense of smugness only really weirdly bright people can feel. It was new and it was fleeting . . . and I liked it. I chose to believe that these blue-blooded Northerners were appropriately impressed that this red-blooded Southerner schooled in the halls of a public institution knew about the Möbius strip, which by the way appears to be a two-dimensional object that is really only a surface with one side and one boundary component. Ladies and gentleman, your tax dollars at work.

But my shining moment of being fully embraced as a member of this freaky smart family did not last. I knew I was in a losing battle the year Brad's mom brought some pictures to share of the Harvard Family Christmas. In one photograph, the Mensa Gene Pool had gathered in the kitchen baking (because isn't baking really all about physics?), preparing their annual holiday cake, or something like that. Said cake was, and I'm serious as a heart attack, shaped like Albert Einstein's *head.* They used coconut for the hair and mustache, and I recall they had written $E = MC^2$ with licorice at the bottom of the cake. It really did look like ol' Al, and the entire clan thought it was hysterically funny and wonderful–so much so that they gathered for a family photo around that kooky coconut cake and e-mailed it to the rest of the family, who also thought it was hysterically funny and wonderful. Wow. Please note that my aunt makes a killer coconut cake that requires much labor, four cake pans, and poking holes in the top of it with a wooden spoon handle so all that divine coconut icing stuff can seep down into it. One year she did liken it to a bunny at Easter, but that was it. Yes, I was a square peg in a perfectly round and brilliant hole.

But I like my mother-in-law, I really do. And I know that she likes me, as I am the mother of two of her favorite grandchildren. It took some time for us to get used to one another. But she is so head over heels in love with my kids that she is blinded to my many and deep flaws. Nothing else seems to matter except that I brought forth to her these two wonderful children.

You will not be surprised to know that there are never more than six or eight people (mostly adults, so it's pretty easy to make the cut for the adult table) at Brad's family gatherings. We eat politely at a dining room table formally decorated with nice linen, fine china, sparkling crystal, and sterling silver. There is some sort of roasted meat, a starchy casserole, a vegetable dish, and some very appropriate bread of some sort. There is wine (yippee) and a pie (usually store bought, which is so *wrong*!). Everyone participates in the same scintillating and high-brow conversation at the same time, and no one is yelling or laughing too loud or asking for an extra helping of pinto beans in a coffee cup (sprinkle some butter and cornbread on the top, if you don't mind). You can't get lost in the shuffle in this small crowd, and you certainly have to pull your own weight in conversation.

Brad could not be more at home at this table, and I could not be more homesick. And while there are not tons of divorced people in his family, there are some. Brad's parents, for example. In fact, Brad's parents chose Christmastime to tell him and his two siblings they were getting a divorce. He was nine. While they all knew it wasn't Ozzie and Harriet around the Muller household, it still came as a shock. All three children reacted as you would expect–tears, disbelief, uncertainty. Yet somehow this experience never took the joy out of Christmas for my husband. He clung to memories of jumping on his grandparents' bed. Emptying stockings on Christmas morning. The big family breakfast. The mountain of presents that seemed to take hours to open. Somehow, he managed to hang on to some semblance of his holiday spirit. Maybe that's why he is the Christmas Tree Stud.

So whether there are six or sixteen gathering at the holiday table, we all have visions of a Christmas celebration with the perfect sheen and patina. We spend weeks planning the menu, wrapping the gifts, and fluffing the house. And of course, finding the perfect holiday card to send to more than two hundred of your closest family and friends. The whole holiday family photo card has become its own cottage industry, and is reaching new and ridiculous heights (not to mention expense). Parents are scoping photo ops throughout the year . . . "Collage" cards are my favorite to receive, as they invite you to take a trip(s) with the family: Here we are at Disneyland at our behind-the-scenes tour of Cinderella's Castle; then off to Aspen to ski (yes, do note the black diamond signage in the background); oh, let's not forget the beach where we parasailed for the first time; here we are swimming with endangered orcas; then here are various candids of our incredibly successful and well-adjusted kids at various sporting and athletic events (soccer, baseball, jazz, and swim team). And let's top it all off with a great church photo just to showcase how good the kids look squeaky clean and holy. Yep, no matter the season, here we are in all our picture-perfect glory. We choreograph not only the most perfect holidays, but also the entire year.

Lest I seem a hypocrite, we do send out a holiday card, with just one photo, of the kids only. But I always wondered what it would be like to send a holiday collage card of "Real Life with Charla." The photo collage would consist of the following:

> Here is Mom cleaning up cat barf off the living room carpet and yelling that if the litter box doesn't get changed this instant, the cat will go "bye-bye, and for real this time!"

Here is Mom taking out the garbage and recycling bins in the rain. She is in clogs, a floral house robe, a few odd hot rollers, and a beach hat (to camouflage the rollers, of course) and looks so stunningly ridiculous that running into the Neighbor She Would Most Dread Running Into is practically a given. Oh look, there she is now.

And here is Mom half-dressed and late for church and arguing with her family whether we will stay for Big Church or just go to Sunday School. Say Cheese!

Happy Freakin' Holidays. Love (A Little), Char

I was thirty-three years old before I woke up in my own bed, in my own house, *my own* house, with Brad and my daughter, on Christmas morning. It was "Brad's year" for Christmas and we would see his family that afternoon. You would think I would have treasured this long-awaited day as if it were that special Christmas gift I never received as a kid. (Remember the 10-speed bike, Mom and Dad?) But in many ways it was disappointing–the quiet was deafening when I was used to opening presents among a cacophony of cousins, aunts, uncles, and grandparents. Breakfast was a tad boring when I was used to a table crammed with people, eggs, ham, bacon, biscuits, and way too many jars of homemade jam. While I was thrilled to be with the people whom I loved most–my husband and daughter–I was a holiday chaos junkie and I needed a fix. Even Brad felt it was a little anticlimactic. After all, there are only so many pictures you can take of a two-year-old tugging at wrapping paper who is more interested in the box and bow than the toy that came in it. It was all just a little . . . bit . . . off.

One of the very few fights Brad and I have ever had was about Santa. It was our daughter's first Christmas and we were working on Santa and his presentation. Because as we all know, presentation is *everything*, even for an infant. "Well, when are we going to wrap everything?" Brad asked one evening before the Big Day.

"Everything is already wrapped," I replied.

"And here is the Santa stuff," I said, pointing to a pile of unwrapped gifts in the corner of the guest bedroom.

"No," he said. "We need to wrap Santa. Everyone always wraps Santa."

Are you *high*? No one, I mean *no one* in *my* family or in *my* circle of friends from *my* town or living on *my* planet (called Earth) wraps gifts from Santa. What a colossal hassle! What a waste of drugstore wrapping paper! But apparently, in the World According to Brad, all Santa gifts are wrapped, including tiny little stocking stuffers . . . down to a tube of lip balm, thank you very much. I was dumbfounded. I could not get my head around the logic or the need to wrap Santa's presents. I mean, isn't that gilding the Santa?

"Hon," I said, trying my best to bring some common sense to the discussion. "We don't need to wrap Santa. After we open gifts on Christmas Eve, Santa's unwrapped presents will magically appear under the tree for Virginia and she'll squeal in delight when she enters the room, and we'll capture it all on film for future generations. It will be great."

Brad sat up straight, and got that weird chin-jut thing going that tells me I'm in for a long night on this one. "For starters, we *don't* open presents on Christmas Eve, and second, we wrap *all* of Santa, and third, we all come downstairs and each calmly empty our stockings. Then we break for a family breakfast, and then we open the gifts under the tree, and then we head to church." I eventually stopped listening. I couldn't *believe* I had married a man who had lived this way! I mean, who orchestrated Christmas at his house–Stalin? It all sounded torturous and miserable.

And while I had some idea we would have to negotiate things like finances and religion, who knew Santa tradition was a religion all its own? I mean, I could have told Brad I was naming our daughter after my ex-boyfriend's golden retriever and he would have put up less of a fuss. "So if you don't open gifts on Christmas Eve, what do you do? Wait," I said. "I don't really want to know." It probably involved shoveling snow, cutting wood, or knitting scarves for prisoners. Well, in *my* family, we open all family gifts on Christmas Eve, open Santa gifts (sans wrapping paper) on Christmas morning, and that's that.

I vaguely recalled in the back of my mind all that advice about how couples have to very conscientiously come together as a new and different family unit, but I didn't wanna! I wanted to do it my way. And my way is *my* family and *my* version of Christmas and *my* chaos. And it really stank that I didn't get my way. In the end, we agreed that we would open family gifts on Christmas Eve and that Santa would be wrapped. As a concession, Brad promised to wrap all Santa gifts, down to a tube of toothpaste for a stocking stuffer. This effort required a different set of wrapping paper kept hidden away under lock and key lest smart little minds think, "Hey, that's weird, Santa has the same wrapping paper as Mom!" We've been wrapping Santa tediously–large and small–for the last eight years, and while it certainly is a tradition now at our house, it still feels a little . . . bit . . . off.

The pressure of Christmas and the psychotic need to adhere to what we know (even if it's dumb and restrictive and doesn't make a lick of sense) and to resist what we don't know run deep in us all. Wrapping Santa . . . spending every Thanksgiving, Christmas, and Easter at your grandmother's house . . . decorating the Christmas tree. We all carve out our own truth in life, I guess, much like my grandparents did. Because *all* families are flawed and dysfunctional and often crazy–despite their picture-perfect holiday cards. And really, that is all we know. And if the flaws and dysfunction and craziness are deeply rooted in affection, love, and gentle humor–then isn't that all that matters? And this year, we've added a new tradition of sorts to our house: Every night the Christmas Tree Stud and Charla Scrooge crawl into bed together and have a warm, cozy, sexy cuddle. And when we don't, that's when things feel just . . . a little bit . . . off.

JANUARY

New Year's Resolutions and the Seven-Month Itch

"Brad, it's not like I minded, but do you think it's strange that we didn't do it on New Year's Eve? Isn't New Year's Eve like the mother of all 'if we're gonna do it, New Year's Eve is the night' night?"

"Oh, I don't know. New Year's Eve is so overrated," Brad said dismissively. He continued, "When you're standing in a mud puddle, picking at a wedding cake comprised entirely of Krispy Kreme Doughnuts, it kind of kills the mood for anything but a warm bed and lots of Tylenol."

"Well, New Year's does seem like an important 'have sex' event," I argued, feeling off-kilter. In the past, I would have felt obligated to have sex with Brad on New Year's; now I'm out of whack when we aren't having sex on New Year's Eve. Is that crazy, or what?

"Are you kidding me?" Brad said defensively. "We have such an unbelievable sex life right now, even I'm amazed and I'm living it. Needing to have sex on New Year's seems kind of amateurish."

* * *

We did not have sex on New Year's Eve. All over the world, frisky drunk people got lucky, but my husband cashed in his sex-every-day chip for some hard-earned sleep.

New Year's Eve was rung in at a wedding. Our invitation was a bit of dumb luck, but it enabled Brad and me to continue the long-standing tradition of spending New Year's Eve with my mom and dad (and my brother and his wonderful wife). Before you start snickering about a grown woman who still likes to ring in the New Year with Dick and the 'rents, I'd like to note that hanging out with my parents is always an upgrade for Brad and me. We travel in style, we always have a great time, and I'm one of those people who find their parents and their parents' friends a whole lot of fun.

Last year, we ended up at a black-tie affair at my parents' club with about forty couples over the age of eighty. We were mildly amused but also somewhat embarrassed, until my sister-in-law convinced us it was just like being on a cruise ship. We just needed to focus on our table–the Captain's Table, of course–and no one else mattered. And once we changed our focus, my brother and I continued our long-standing tradition of our New Year's Dance-Off, where we compete for top honors in front of a team of judges made up of parents, spouses, and me. And once again, big sister won.

So in light of the previous year's debacle of "let's pretend we're on a cruise ship and it will all be okay," a New Year's Eve wedding did promise to be wonderfully romantic–black tie, dancing, friends, family, and a Krispy Kreme wedding cake.

But it was not meant to be–cold rain of biblical proportions blew sideways into the wedding tent (yes, friends, this was an outdoor wedding in the mountains in January, and no, I don't know what they were thinking either).

With a heated tent the size of an Olympic skating arena, a live band, and clever catering, it was an entertaining evening . . . until nature intervened. Between the cavernous party tent and the Porta Pottis was an area that collected rainwater at an alarming rate. I know what you're thinking–black tie and Porta Pottis, just don't mix–but these Porta Pottis were little chalets, complete with running water and a small, fogged-up mirror in which to check exactly how heinous one's hair looked after running from the car to the church, from the church to the car, and from the car to the reception tent in sideways rain. (For the record, I did look pretty heinous with my hair frizzed out and damp strappy party shoes, but who cares what I looked like? I'm not the gal in white, and she looked terrific and amazingly dry.) On the way back from his own lively jaunt in the pouring rain, Brad made a misguided step into a mud hole so deep it sucked off his shoe. After limping around the reception with his wet pant leg slapping back and forth like a broken windshield wiper, he couldn't wait to get home, out of his wringing wet tux and soggy wingtips, and into bed. He was sleeping like the dead before I even finished toweling off. So there was no scoring that night, but a nice little snuggle to regain body heat, and some roof-raising snoring. (Ah, love.)

On the way home, however, in the back of my brother's "come to the Dark Side" minivan loaded with four other people, we had a backseat smooch session like we were teenagers. This, I had to admit, was not normal behavior for us. In the past it would have been a warm embrace and a meaningful peck and let's call it a day. But it seems that touch begets touch, and regular intimacy makes everything nice. So this little high school moment was a great way to ring in the New Year–a little whipped cream to top off the already sweet holidays. In fact, intimacy every day makes everything sweeter . . . even on those occasional days when my husband takes a pass in favor of a boozy night's sleep. But imagine the bride and groom and the pressure they will forever feel to have sex on New Year's Eve . . . because it's their wedding anniversary and the eve of a new year. I mean the stress of a celebration *à deux*.

We had entered the New Year cold, wet, and hungover–not an ideal start. So after we returned from the wedding, it was time to hit the ground running. New Year = New Me! Although this sounds inspirational and fresh, really, I was falling into a pattern often repeated. I got busy setting unattainable resolutions, *again*, and Brad vowed, *again*, not to make any at all. Brad leads his life on the straight and narrow, which means he doesn't fall for wild makeover ideas or wacky resolutions. This makes him a wee bit of a killjoy when it comes to brainstorming resolutions that we can pick and execute *together*. Me? I'm bouncing off resolutions like a pinball: "Let's give up red meat!" I would exclaim. "Let's journal every day together!" "Let's start a supper club!" "Let's meditate together!" "Let's take a landscaping class!" "Let's give up television!"

"Hey, why don't we just have a lot of sex?" Brad wryly suggested. Party pooper . . .

We'd had six months of sex *almost* every day (I'm still trying to get over that New Year's thing), and had become the poster couple for predictable sex: mostly at night, after the kids had gone to sleep, or in earlier hours, depending on our families' schedules, or before a date night out. Perhaps we could have pulled out a copy of the *Kama Sutra* looking for some inspiration to mix things up a bit. But I think we were too exhausted by our busy lives now pumped up on daily sex steroids to care, although my husband would never, ever admit it.

Since July, we had gone from 0 to 100 miles per hour in the sex department, and I worried whether it was even possible to keep things exciting and new. In the old days, PG (pre–The Gift), that something new was actually just *having* sex. The bitter truth now seven months into it was that I didn't have the energy to create any huge, romantic encounters to kick things up a notch, and lead us out of the land of run-of-the-mill sex to the kingdom of earth-shattering, knock your socks off, wake the neighbors that was so awesome! That kind of encounter would be really great to have, just as having a mouthwatering three-course gourmet dinner every night would be terrifically sinful and decadent . . . *but it's just not gonna happen.* Because when I suggested sex every day, I envisioned it being short, sweet, and well . . . sweet. Not long, sweaty, and labor-intensive (which kind of sounds like childbirth, actually). In our hectic lives, who has the time for that kind of creativity . . . or work?

I rationalized: Wasn't just having sex, basic and routine as it might be, good enough? Brad certainly wasn't complaining. It's like the wonder of getting basic cable when you've had only three channels for most of your life–it's still an upgrade, right? Besides, I had all these other resolutions distracting me . . . creating award-winning photo albums for my kids to treasure for the rest of their lives, learning how to work my new kick-butt KitchenAid industrial mixer (with so many weird attachments it could have sex with my husband), losing weight (again), and eating better (as always).

So I guess when scrapbooking and losing weight began to take up more space in my mind than canoodling with Brad, it was official. Raise the flag, folks: *We had hit the seven-month itch.* Intimacy is no longer interesting and I'm not really interested in making it interesting. Which begs the question, can you have too much sex? Is it like diluting lemonade with too much water; it's not as satisfying? If you eat a pound of M&Ms, does it make you not want to eat M&Ms for a while?

Some would argue that, for men, sex seems like such a necessary physical relief that it never could be diluted. Some husbands claim that they might suffer and die from DSB–otherwise known as Deadly Sperm Buildup–if they don't get some action. Now I'd like to know what these husbands (not mine, mind you) think might happen–would their heads blow off their bodies? Would they suffer from that other urban myth (you know what I'm talking about)? Would they start bleeding out of their eyeballs? *Please.* On the flip side, experts contend that guys can have too much sex and girls can't. Really? I have a hard time believing that, but this study is referencing the physical implications of having lots and lot of sex (which impacts guys' anatomy), not the complete and utter emotional drain of having lots and lots of sex (which clearly impacts me). Intimacy every day is good; at least it has been so far. But I have to admit that it's getting harder to do all that I have to do every day and still have enough energy to tackle a little session with Brad.

So, I decided to try and mesh my New Year's Resolutions with my own Sexual Revolution. Since January is the month of fresh starts, of atoning for holiday sins and getting healthy, eating better, and losing weight, this seemed like a logical step. To keep me going, I set out on the path to find out just how sex could make me accomplish almost all of my goals (except for getting my kids' scrapbook done). Was it possible that daily sex could make me slimmer, happier, and healthier? Could I knock out all my resolutions with one well-executed nightly encounter? Well, I would find out. And in the meantime, just to be safe, I joined a gym along with the rest of America.

Being a woman with a part-time job, full-time kids, husband, house, and the unrelenting gift of intimacy . . . and now a workout appointment, I couldn't really dive into any scholarly Ph.D.-level research. I didn't have the staff, the grant money, the laboratory, the university library, or six years of free time to find willing participants to pull levers, get wired up, and answer copious amounts of questions. Instead, I had a mom's best friend: Google, for online research; a DVR, to capture those three-minute chunks of bullet-pointed wisdom from the morning TV shows; and a husband, with whom I was having sex every day for a year (who needs lab rats?). Based on these piecemeal and hackneyed bits of research I could cull during my spare time, I discovered quite a bit:

Our Gift Was Making Me Healthier. Sex burns calories and that is always, always, always a good thing. In fact, a good romp can burn up to two hundred calories, which is the same as a candy bar. So could I trade off a trek to the gym for a roll in the hay? Well, some researchers said yes, and some killjoy realist said no, that, unless you're having a thirty- to forty-five-minute session of lovin' and maintaining an appropriately elevated heart rate, it's not gonna cut it. Brad and I, as previously noted, ahem, aren't competing at that Olympic level. Wouldn't it be great, though, if all those people who swarmed the gyms and health clubs on January second with their newly laminated membership cards were instead at home boogying with their spouse to get fit? There would be no need for pricey new workout gear, a gym membership, an iPod, or couples therapy (down the road). Simply hop in the sack and get healthy.

One of my girlfriends likens having sex to going to the gym. "You know it's the right thing to do. You dread it, but once you get there, you're glad you're there, and you're happy you did it. And I never regret doing it." As I've mentioned before and as most of my girlfriends agree, there has never been a time when I've been intimate with Brad and later thought, "Well, that was a complete waste of time." Rather, it's quite yummy. I personally hate going to the gym, so this analogy rings painfully true for me. In fact, I could live for another fifty years and not ever step foot inside a gym again and die happy (although probably too soon). But I'll keep going, especially as it might help rev up the hormones, so I can feel some of that drive that men feel. My friend Sarah told me a story about her friend who suddenly became a fitness buff over the summer: It could be from some sort of increased testosterone that comes with working out, but her husband is laughingly complaining that she can't get enough lovin', and now she's hunting him down for sex. So it's a win-win–she's getting healthy, feeling sexy, and getting sex.

Joining the gym this time around wasn't half as bad as I had remembered, but I did wait until the end of the month so it didn't seem so flagrantly formulaic. This particular gym met my two key criteria–cheap and low-key. It was not a scene, and in fact it was so low-key it didn't really have a name . . . or if it did, I didn't know it. It was not listed in the phone book and only two trainers worked there. It was in a low-slung generic warehouse in an industrial part of town. There was no signage, so I had to follow someone over there the first time I went. There was nothing to call it, so I dubbed it the Underground Gym. I had several girlfriends who *swore* by the Underground Gym and one trainer's transforming thirty-minute workouts, and the ridiculously reasonable fees.

I had to admit these gals looked great. So I gave it a shot. My girlfriends warned me that the first sessions were rough. "Don't freak," they said. The first day my friend and I went, we did an unseemly number of squats on a minitramp along with some other lower body torture.

My workout buddy called me the next day. "How are you?" she asked.

"Is this some kind of sick joke?" I screamed into the phone. I had done what my friends had warned against–I freaked. "I can't even go to the bathroom!" I wailed. "Once I sit down, I can't get up . . . I'm dying from squat pain!"

"Me too! Are you going back?" she asked.

"Well, they say the worst is behind us, unless I die on the loo and Brad finds me there . . . yeah, I guess I'll go back." And two days and seventy-two ibuprofen later I was back at the Underground Gym begging for more. I was fairly diligent, going two or three times a week–caught up in that strangely pathetic New Year momentum.

But the Underground Gym keeps odd hours, and the trainers kind of set the schedule, so there were days when I came and it was closed, or my trainer wasn't there. One day I asked one of the gals why the trainer took a break at seven in the morning–I mean, that's kind of prime workout time. "Well, he's been here all night and so he goes home and sleeps for a bit." Huh? "Yeah, don't you know? This gym trains some of the dancers from the local clubs after their shift. They come in around three or four in the morning and train." Wow, I let that information slowly seep in. Charla shares a trainer with exotic dancers. Who woulda thunk it? I couldn't believe it either. Kevin Bacon couldn't have recorded a more remarkable connection between two groups of people–only one degree separated the finest exotic dancers in the Carolinas and me, a frumpy thirty-nine-year-old working mom of two. Brad nearly burst his appendix when he heard. "He trains exotic dancers at night? Char, that has got to be the funniest thing I've ever heard," he said. And I admit, it was.

But after a couple of weeks of regular gym time, I can attest to the fact that it's true that when you're feeling healthy, you are more interested in intimacy. I have to admit that I had a little kick in my step, especially when it came to lovin'. In fact, when you're feeling healthy, everything is more interesting. That's why old people are cranky–they simply don't feel good, nothing about their bodies is working right, and they have chronic indigestion. And that's why kids are so happy–they have regular bowel movements, they run around and climb on things, and they sleep a lot. Eating right and exercising are good for us and, likewise (though I never would have bought it if you'd sold me on it eight months ago), so is having sex with our spouses.

One talking head on TV said that time spent with your spouse, doing something that you don't normally do together (which, ironically, before The Gift, would have been having sex), can make you feel good. I wondered whether the day I made my husband go paint pottery (something we normally don't do together and will never, ever do again, according to Brad) could have been "healthy" for our relationship? Well, not really, because all he did was marvel out loud at his incredible misfortune at being stuck in a place that he commented was surely "what hell looks like," which kind of took all the fun out of our "quality-time outing." But I eventually figured out what would be great time spent: We had a great grown-ups-only weekend outing at a winery, and had some scintillating conversation, yummy wine, and some lovely nuzzling. I think I'm noticing a trend here. My regular intimacy was allowing for feelings of health and wellness that begat a desire to have more sex.

Sex Was Making Me Happier. Intimacy is a stress reliever. When there is so much responsibility in keeping the Muller boat afloat, a nice relaxing romp with Brad can be a wonderful respite, and a nice distraction from feeling like the world is going to crumble if I'm not out there battling dragons 24/7. Research I found backs this up, and I would venture to say that men across America (and even across the world) laugh out loud anytime they hear that someone paid lots of money to commission research that tells us that sex relieves stress and can release endorphins that make you feel happy and relaxed.

But as a member of the other gender, I can attest from personal experience that I was pleasantly surprised that my evening encounters would provide such moments. I had spent so much of my time pre–The Gift getting worked up over avoiding sex because the thought of it stressed me out, that I failed to see going on the offensive would serve me (and Brad) much better. After a day that included meeting the house cleaner, hustling to a teacher conference, a lunch meeting, work, and later an after-school party for my daughter that was so wild and chaotic it would drive Mother Teresa to drink, I was too exhausted for sex, but not too tired to try to forget about my hellish day. And in an odd way, that's what is so great about my daily sessions with Bad–for a few minutes I can relax, feel those little endorphins pinging around my body, and forget about my crap of a day. It's much cheaper than a massage, too (I'm a bargain shopper, remember).

Our Intimate Moments Were Making Me Feel Younger. This is

perhaps the best news of all. According to Dr. Roizen and Dr. Oz from the Real Age Institute, if you have a good sex life (and good means hitting those high notes), you can subtract eight punishing years right off your face. Yay! Forty is the new thirty-two in my book, and for Brad, having sex every day makes him practically a youngster. Why does sex keep you young? Well, it's the cumulative effect of exercise, hormones, relaxation, and hopefully an enhanced relationship with your spouse. So the fountain of youth is at hand, every day!

An active, fulfilling sex life with your spouse makes you healthier, happier, and younger, so why in the world didn't I start sooner? Instead of hanging out at the Underground Gym bitterly huffing and puffing through hundreds of sit-ups, why wasn't I hanging out solely in the bedroom? (Believe me, my husband is asking the same question when I complain about my sore quads.) Because if I'm healthier, happier, and younger, then who needs plastic surgery, Botox, and the gym? Oh *wait*, I do need the gym to raise my libido. It looks like I'm going to live longer and look better simply by doing the deed.

My personal trainer is helping me get toned (at least this month)–mastering my squats, strengthening my abs, and increasing my endurance. I wonder if there are personal intimacy coaches out there who might do the same thing. They could help folks master the schedule of intimacy, strengthen their relationship with their spouses, and increase endurance, of course. Wait, it gets better! What if I could track our intimacy schedule online and correlate it with overall household happiness? What if I could increase my sex reps as I gained strength and confidence? And then, finally I could become the lean, mean intimacy machine that I know I can be. Ha.

We all hear and read that sex is fundamentally good for us, but it seems that the benefits surrounding it and reported to us aren't enough to motivate people in long-term relationships. Dodging sex, it turns out, is pretty normal. According to the National Institute of Health, 43 percent of women aged 18–59 have sexual dysfunction (I prefer the word "issues") at some time. Sexual problems can range from lack of interest (check) to lack of arousal (no comment) to–hold on to your panties because it gets worse–the inability even to have sex or to achieve the Big O.

I think the majority of my girlfriends would agree that a lack of interest in sex is something we all contend with at some point or time in the cycle of marriage. While there can be many physical reasons for losing interest in intimacy, there are some important emotional reasons as well.

For example, the "I'm Sorry, Do I Know You?" syndrome (aka a lack of communication between partners). How can we be intimate with a spouse whom we don't see except for five minutes in the morning, while he's in the middle of showering and flossing? It's a struggle to stay in tune with someone who spends more time with his administrative assistant and "team" at the office than with us. And while this can initially be okay because reconnection can be nice, these few and far between moments can lead to feelings of awkwardness around your partner (or your spouse taking up with said administrative assistant).

Other mood killers: "Is it Just Me or Is It Terribly Sad in Here?" (aka depression). Okay, I've had this, and I know that

I need to do as much as I can to keep its cold and clammy hands away from my brain. (See March.) You should, too, if you please can. Depression is a drag on every part of your life, intimacy included.

Then there is the "Hey, Sperm Bank, Come Here" (aka sex = procreation only). Believing sex is only for making babies and then after that nada, no way, no how. And the old "Well, Your Beer Gut is Bigger than My Rear End" (aka fear of being rejected, underperforming, and generally not feeling good about yourself and/or poor self-image). Need I say more?

These are just some of the problems that can lead to intimacy issues. I can attest to experiencing most all of them at one time or another (and while Brad does have a bit of a beer belly during football season, I still think he's cute). And me? Well, this baby does have some back and it's not getting in the way one bit.

But we do go to the mats over his manscaping as I am trying desperately to pull him into the twenty-first-century of personal grooming. We have this big debate regarding nose hair, and Brad's eyebrows' tendency toward the Vincent Price look. Brad is *mortally* wounded when I kindly point out that his nose hair is getting in his food, or when I politely ask how he can read the paper with those caterpillars hovering on his forehead. He thinks I'm being critical and snarky, while I contend I am being helpful and snarky. I mean, if your spouse isn't going to tell you that there is spinach in your teeth or a Velcro roller still stuck in the back of your hair, then tell me, why are they even there? I assure Brad that I do not love him less when his ear hair tickles my arm at night (are you noticing a theme here?). And I assure him that I won't be offended if he tells me that an outfit is "not my best look." Anyway, I digress. I've bought him one of those cool Sharper Image trimmer products, and can only hope that he jumps on the manscaping bandwagon. Now if I could only get him to shave his toes . . .

With all this knowledge, both from my delicate dip into the sea of information out there for all to access and my own personal findings, I decided to make a sex improvement plan. This is kind of like a home improvement plan, but without the appliances. In other words, my plan didn't involve going out and buying "marital aids" from some themed party at my neighbor's house. What this plan did involve was a more thoughtful approach to our sex life. So instead of wasting time wondering what the graveyard shift at the Underground Gym might be like, nibbling on oatmeal egg-white pancakes, or going online to track my weight fluctuation with my Internet coach, I focused on rewarding myself with the information that my gift of intimacy could be an all-in-one health tool. And I discovered that the me who had come up with this idea of daily intimacy was as much a genius as those Ph.D., M.D., grant-given researchers.

I was on the front lines, knee deep in research, and I discovered that our scheduled approach to loving, with a few side trips to places like that winery to mix it up, turned out to be serving us just fine. The benefits and the payoffs, I found, were long-term, wrinkle-reducing, serotonin-enhancing good stuff that added to Brad's super shimmy and feelings of well-being and happiness. And if that wasn't exciting enough, hey, I could always head out to the Underground Gym.

FEBRUARY

The Hallmark Moments

"You know, hon, you have a big birthday coming up next month. Any thoughts on what you might want?" Brad asked me one night.

"Oh, I don't know . . ." I said, dreaming of a day at the spa, being rolled in a seaweed wrap, and listening to oddly soothing New Age music while inhaling lavender.

Brad laughed. "Well, what about sex for a year?"

I sat up, horrified. "Are you kidding me? How about no *sex for a year?"*

He didn't utter another word, shocked at the vehemence of my reply. The happy, amused look on his face was gone.

That was not nice of me, I know. I am well aware this 365-day gift was of my own doing. But while I realized that my response was a bit of an exaggeration, I didn't think I would miss having it *every* day. I was agreeably, if not always happily, committed to our arrangement, but after that? Good question. I certainly didn't want to do this for *another* 365 days, but I also didn't want to go back to having sex just on the Hallmark moments, like birthdays and Valentine's Day . . .

I was turning forty, which for some reason was okay with me. My friend once noted that children don't hit their milestones on the year, but on the half-year. So the Terrible Twos really arrive at two and a half and the Fearless Fours at four and a half and so on. Well, that applies to me, too, although I am taller and only slightly less prone to tantrums. I really got hung up on twenty-five for a lot of silly little reasons. That's when I realized that I really should drop college activities from my résumé, that I was getting carded less and less, and that I could now legally rent a car, which meant that I was officially a *responsible adult.* I then cruised with no problems straight through thirty, but stubbed my toe on thirty-five. That's when the Big Lie (see October) revealed itself to me. So here I am turning forty and it's not that big of a deal. For two reasons: (1) I'm quite distracted these days with that little ol' fortieth birthday gift I gave to Brad; and (2) I figure I'll be in some intense therapy around my forty-fifth birthday, so why not have some fun now?

But I did want a nod to forty and all that we women choose to have it represent, namely that it is the new thirty. So, instead of sex every day for a year, Brad and the kids took me to my favorite local Italian restaurant. We had 6 P.M. reservations and were the only ones in the place. The children presented me with homemade cards, and I got some lovely earrings from Brad. It was perfect.

I am not high maintenance when it comes to gifts, which is a good thing because Brad doesn't always give gifts well (although I love the earrings). He's very giving in many ways, just not in a gift-giving way. And I'm kinda picky about some things, so it makes the whole gift deal difficult to master. I would hate to dictate–go to this store and ask for this sales clerk who has these things on hold and buy them. I recognize that I am my own worst gift-giving enemy. So I know that I probably won't receive some lavish, "It's perfect, how did you know?" gift on my birthday or Valentine's Day. It's just not in our cards as a couple. As a result, I am mildly amused and somewhat suspect when I see women point to every bauble on their body as a prize earned: "This necklace was Valentine's Day 2002, this ring was Baby Number 1; the earrings were Christmas 2004; this broach was from our fifth anniversary; and the bracelet was from my appendectomy last spring. (Oh, and that navel ring is from spring break my junior year.)"

And then there are some gals who will give a play-by-play on the events of their birthday, which included breakfast in bed, flowers delivered, a special meal prepared, presents galore, surprise spa treatments, phone calls from around the world, a gourmet dinner and champagne toasts, and so on. It becomes a kind of crazy, keeping-up-with-the-Joneses competition to see whose husband can pronounce his undying love through expensive gifts and special indulgences. Are we all hooked on those little trophies we receive to mark the passage of our lives, and are we missing something more special by expecting or even demanding gifts instead of something deeper? Who knows. Personally, I'm all about balance, so a nice bauble and some heartfelt connection are perfect.

Does a woman think that her husband loves her more because he buys her diamonds? Probably not. Is money spent at a jewelry store proof of love that's not shown in other ways? Maybe. Do we hope a diamond really is forever and that it will carry over to our marriage? It's funny, but not one of my girlfriends has ever said, "I got the best gift ever–the most amazing night of jaw-dropping sex from my husband in honor of Valentine's Day." Not one. And I don't believe it's because my girlfriends are shy about talking about that sort of thing either. I just don't think it happens. It certainly wasn't my experience with Brad–I wasn't racing home with fingers crossed hoping for a wonderfully memorable tryst. So now I can say, "I got this ring when I got married and these earrings when I turned forty." And I also had a wonderful intimate evening with my husband of nearly ten years.

I wouldn't decline baubles, trinkets, cards, and flowers, mind you, but they're not required. Perhaps that's because Brad scores high in the communications department (for a guy), and is generous with notes, cards, and phone calls, and even an occasional bouquet throughout the year. Gift giving aside, we've never had to lean on *the most important romantic holiday of the year* to connect.

Valentine's Day is overrated. Well, when you're single, it's overrated, because you loathe seeing everybody paired up like they're headed for Noah's Ark, and you feel the rain pouring down. When you're married, it feels redundant–romance is so *yesterday*. We're together now, and don't have to jump through hoops with each other, right? Or is it because once you're married, every day is Valentine's Day? (I know, I'm giggling, too.) Well, that's what I used to think when I was a young, brash newlywed. I thought every day would be one giant lovey-dovey of a day–full of sweet murmurings, indulgent glances, and lusty embraces. This can be added to the abysmally long list of things that I didn't know about the real world of marriage.

Even so, after ten years together, Valentine's Day is a holiday that does require a thoughtful nod and a sweet embrace–so that *I* don't seem like a heartless wench and *Brad* doesn't seem like a total cad. Then, we're done. Besides, at this stage in our lives, it's a challenge to celebrate Valentine's Day in a manner that's befitting of Hallmark, FTD, and every romantic bistro drumming for business. Is it even possible to get a babysitter on *the most important romantic holiday of the year*? Nope. Is it even possible to get a reservation at those cute restaurants on *the most romantic holiday of the year*? No. Is it even possible to deliver roses that won't wilt within hours of receipt on *the most important romantic holiday of the year*? Of course not.

Don't get me wrong. I appreciate the sentiment of Valentine's Day and the idea of reaching out to those you love. But these days, I spend upward of fifty bucks on cards for grandparents, aunts, uncles, cousin, babysitters and other folks who might drift onto the radar during *the most important romantic holiday of the year.* So, yes, for me the holiday–which for some reason seems to last a week at my kids' schools–is a bit overrated. The artificial nature of forcing everybody to be romantic and loving on Valentine's Day, along with the logistics of doing anything on this one anointed day, has forced Brad and me to be creative. For example:

> Before kids, we took turns cooking for each other. Romantic? Sure. But in reality, this was because on one occasion Brad waited too long and couldn't land us a reservation anywhere in town. Thus, a tradition was born for the Mullers.
>
> We go out to dinner on a night *other* than Valentine's Day. Practical *and* romantic! We can avoid the crowds and the cheesy gestures–like the restaurant laying a red rose next to your mint when you pay the bill.
>
> We go out to dinner with another couple. Weird, but true. All two-tops in town are booked on the fourteenth, but try for a four-top or an eight-top and, *voilà*, you're in! Plus,

most of our friends find the holiday to be as contrived and corny as we do, so we make fun and have a good time.

We stay home and cook with our kids, and feast on a dessert of their candy. Valentine's Day rivals Halloween in the amount of candy my kids receive–it's so weird–whatever happened to giving just plain Scooby Doo cards at school? Now half the kids attach red-hot hearts, candy hearts, chocolates, Tootsie Pops–you name it and it's now repackaged in pink and red. And like Halloween candy, much of it *I* eat or it goes bad and I throw it out while the kids are at school.

But for Brad's very special year, we had to do something, right? So we opted to battle the masses and use a gift card Brad had received at an upscale steakhouse in town. So steakhouses aren't romantic bistros, but the food is outstanding, and hey, we had a gift card. And the Force was with us because we scored a sitter (my mother-in-law). So we set out for a romantic dinner for two, along with everyone else in the city.

This was my first time at the Steakhouse That Shall Remain Nameless. While lots of women enjoy ordering dainty salads of mixed mesclun (which is code for lettuce weed that gets stuck between your teeth), I not only eat to live, but eat to enjoy. And I always enjoy a good piece of rare red meat.

So we're sitting at a table for two, next to a salon-coiffed high school couple in their prom duds (which makes me feel quite old) and the rest of the motley assortment of people who thought it was a good idea to go out to dinner with the thousands of other people going out to dinner on *the most romantic holiday of the year.* And we order our steaks. Which come à la cart, so we order some asparagus–which is really five freakishly fat stalks of asparagus for fourteen dollars.

Then our waiter casually asks: "And would you like to add on a lobster tail with your steak, sir? We have one petite tail and three jumbo tails left. I would be happy to reserve one for you . . ." "No thank you," says Brad. But after every menu exchange, our waiter deftly inserts again, "And would you like to add on a lobster tail with your steak, sir? We have one petite tail and three jumbo tails left. I would be happy to reserve one for you." He does this three or four more times. He is very smooth. To which, I finally coo, "Oh, honey, why not? You love lobster and it's just an add-on. Let's do it. We have a gift card and all!" And so he does. And the petite tail add-on is a nice, little four-ounce chunk of lobster. It's about four or five bites, but it's perfectly cooked.

And do you know what? After our bill arrives, we find out that sweet little lobster tail add-on, which the waiter so kindly reserved on our behalf, costs forty-five freakin' dollars! It's more than our pan-seared at 1800 degrees filet mignon! Clearly, we have been had. I do not doubt the sincerity of our waiter, but shame on me for not asking the price and shame on him for not offering. I think there should be a rule–if a waiter is trying to upsell you an item that costs more than the most expensive steak on the menu, then he should be required to tell you the cost.

Well, it doesn't matter, as that restaurant is Officially Dead to Me. I will never step one well-pedicured toe in there ever again. It doesn't really matter to Brad, because he goes there all the time with customers. He can get his fix on a steak seared at 1800 degrees and I don't even have to know.

To conclude our night, and get over the lobster tail debacle, we go home and have a roll in the hay. And I have to say *that* is the highlight of *the most important romantic holiday of the year.* And as well it should be.

We had kind of promoted ourselves out of predictable "milestone" sex by having sex every day. Milestone sex is the pressure to have sex on birthdays, anniversaries, and other romantic times such as Valentine's Day.

But for those not dipping their toes into the pool of intimacy as often, some clever person (hey, it could be me!) could promote sex considerably by encouraging people to have sex on major holidays. You know, instead of "The Jeweler's Mother's Day Heart Pendant," we could market the Mother's Day Quickie. In fact, an entire campaign could be developed celebrating trysting on all major and minor holidays. January: New Year's Eve Day and Martin Luther King Day. February: Valentine's Day and President's Day. March: St. Patrick's Day and March Madness. April: Easter and Administrative Professionals Day. May: Mother's Day and Memorial Day. June: Father's Day and Summer Solstice. July: Canada Day and Independence Day. And so on.

You get the Tryst Gist . . . my point is you could feasibly have sex twice a month simply celebrating holidays. Toss in two birthdays and two anniversaries (come on, doesn't everyone celebrate their *engagement* anniversary, per those marketing geniuses at Hallmark?) and you've just added one more session every quarter. For a total of twenty-eight sessions of intimacy a year. Prior to The Gift, Brad would have thought that number agreeable. I'll bet a lot of husbands would.

As you may have noticed, Valentine's Day is no longer a big romantic time for me–instead it's more of a hurdle I have to clear. But as I sat next to that big-haired high school couple at the expensive steakhouse that is now Dead to Me, it stirred a longing for those feelings of anticipation, angst, and sweaty palms that that couple probably had. As much as we like to think that boys and girls aren't even interested in one another until puberty hits, that was not true for me. I knew a cute boy when I saw one–hello, Chris Higgins, in Mrs. Hopkins's first-grade class! And then desires escalate through middle school, high school, college, and into the work world. It's impossible for me to deny that the early days of falling in love were pretty spectacular, and while I'm thrilled to be out of the dating scene and was very happy to "settle down," don't you just miss it sometimes?

That's why I think women are suckers for the old standbys: romance novels, movies, and all the scuttlebutt about work colleagues–we like to vicariously relive those feelings through the stories of other people. But we're always a bit crestfallen when our romantic leads actually get together and settle down: I mean, *Cheers* was never really the same after Sam and Diane got together, was it? Jane Austen was very smart to have the marriage of Elizabeth Bennett and Fitzwilliam Darcy from *Pride and Prejudice* end the book. And watercooler gossip is always about the single people (or people who are having affairs)–because the chase is more exciting than the contentment that comes after "I do."

Young love is inherently crazy and passionate and unpredictable. Old, married love is dependable, without drama, and probably very predictable. What is there to talk about if you're happily married? Yes, he'll probably call. And yes, he'll probably come home tonight. Yes, you'll probably see him over the weekend. And yes, he'll want to have sex because husbands always do. But life was full of drama back in the single days–not life-or-death stuff, but for a single girl, there's a lot of self-involved drama. Will he call and wish me a Happy Birthday? Will he send flowers or a card? Should I call him? (The answer is most always no.) My girlfriends would call to see if he called me, and then we would spend hours dissecting whether he did or didn't. And if he didn't, I would turn to my brilliant friend Julia.

Julia would take hours–hours!–out of her life to help you psychoanalyze a romantic situation (or a situation that you wanted desperately to recount as romantic). She would ask very detailed questions. She would take notes. She would look at your situation from every angle. She would bring to bear her great analytical skills to help you figure out whether that casual "Hey, how you doin'?" at the Pub that night was fraught with great meaning and import, and could be translated into: "I feel this incredible connection over a Miller Lite. I must have you and I will *not* be denied!"

Julia was great at reading body language, verbal cues, and eye movement. Seriously, she should have been a Crush P.I. with all the time she spent as a behavior expert. But I've come to realize that she gave the male gender *way* too much credit and, as a result, I believed that I might have actually had a chance with any number of crushes I developed over the years, which turned out to be just a "Hi, how are ya?" God bless her, she is a very good friend to single women. We should all be so lucky to have a Julia. But now, more than ever, is when I need her help and counsel. Because I feel like dating was the minor leagues. Staying happily married is the big leagues.

Those thrilling feelings of newness, a first-day-of-school anticipation about what might lie ahead, dreaming about how wonderful my life will be when Mr. Terrific and I finally bump into each other, are gone. I've met him, we fell in love, and now we're married. Those luxurious dreams never included bleach sticks, broken garage doors, and sick cats. There seems to be a statute of limitations on new love and you can never recapture the giddy anticipation that comes with it. The cycle runs its course from meeting to falling in love to commitment and then to contentment and to . . . what now?

Giddy anticipation aside, dating for me really did stink; I just remember it with fondness. Much like I remember my freshman year with fondness–without any details–just blurry, slightly out-of-focus recollections. Such as how I smelled like bacon my first semester because my roommate cooked all her food in our dorm room, claiming she "was poisoned by some ham in the dining hall." To remember dating in Technicolor would require me to remember all the dorky things I did/said/thought while hoping to run into the Right Guy. Like the time I was a full-time employee and went out a few times with a college intern and the whole department found out. In my defense, he was only a few years younger and we were just having fun at the Paul Simon concert in Central Park. Man, I never lived that down.

I do not remember meeting my own husband. Had I written it like the start to a Lifetime movie, it might have happened like this:

> "Oh, we met at a Starbucks! He was smitten with the way I ordered my tall, skim, decaf latte."
>
> "We met at the wine store. He knew me from the gym but thought it was just too cheesy to approach me over there." (That one's true and he was right.)
>
> "I picked him up on an airplane. He was 6A, and I was 6C, with nobody in 6B."
>
> "My mother set him up with my sister and then he met me." (This actually happened to my father's two sisters and it was bad, bad, bad, I tell you, and it *would* make a *great* Lifetime movie.)

But back to the *real* story. We met at work, like so many couples do. I interviewed Brad, took him to lunch, and perhaps even returned him to the airport, where he flew home to DC to a job, an apartment, and a girlfriend. I have no recollection of any of this. (He's reminded me.) I don't even know whether I recommended we hire him or not. However, I do remember that I had good hair at the time, a closet full of amazing designer handbags, and I worked out regularly, so you can see I remember the important things.

For our second meeting (which appeared to me like the first time), it was Brad's first day at the agency. Interestingly, we didn't go to lunch–the first lunch was so dang memorable, why chance it? He seemed nice to me as he got settled into our morning briefing, but sad. You know, kind of quiet and remote. As an off-the-charts extrovert, I don't get quiet, remote people, so I just assume they're sad . . . certainly they're not this way *all the time.*

It turned out he *was* sad. He took a job in Charlotte for a clean start from an old life that hadn't worked out. New city, new job, new life. He knew not a soul in Charlotte, but had a sister in South Carolina. He rented a dingy apartment on Albemarle Road because no one counseled him that one should never *ever* rent a dingy apartment on Albemarle Road.

He was overqualified for the job, but he claimed that this new start had presented itself at a key time and he took a risk. I would find out later that he was a quiet and studied risk taker and that most, but not all, of the risks he had taken had worked out quite well to his advantage.

I found out more about him as I took the lead and shopped his tall, eligible self around to my cute, single girlfriends. He worked for the State Department during the first (and much better) Bush administration. He interviewed with the CIA but opted out when they questioned his ability to go for days without sleep and to survive in the wild (he's from Cleveland, after all). He had traveled to a dozen foreign countries, and he enjoyed Aruba much more than Pakistan. He was smart, deliberate, and handsome, and I was not remotely interested in him. I had been through that whole *dating in the workplace* drama once and it had ended as they always do–with lots of tears, painful work meetings, and us doing "rock, scissors, paper" to see who would look for another job. Since I worked there first, we didn't really "rock, scissors, paper" for it; he left for St. Louis and I swore off dating guys from work. Once bitten, twice smart, or so I thought.

Vowing not to get burned again, I had adopted Brad as a project. I had some fun girlfriends, an active social life, and a desire to "help." I set him up with friends, I took him along to the Pub, I invited him to sporting events, I offered some fashion advice (he was from Cleveland, after all), and I gave him obnoxiously detailed updates on my love life with the hope that he might give some advice on the opposite sex.

"So, do you think he'll call?"

"Who?"

"You know, my Crush! I decided not to penalize him for wearing a turtleneck with a sport coat to a basketball game. Do you think he'll call?"

"I have no idea. Does he know you're interested?" he asked patiently.

"Of course not! That would ruin everything!"

Brad indulged me in hearing about my neurotic immature Crushes and mind-numbingly boring tirades about whether the Crush du Jour would call. And I made sure he got on the invite list for some great parties, and strongly counseled him against wearing high-top basketball shoes without socks. It was more than a fair trade-off, I'd say.

Brad helped me move into my first house. Brad helped me with a particularly challenging work colleague (code for she was a heinous witch and I wanted to claw out her eyeballs every time we passed in the hallway). Brad coached me through some more lame Crushes. And on his own time, he made his own friends, nabbed his own invitations to some great parties, trained for a marathon, and blossomed into this incredibly interesting person. My friend Christy contended that he was this incredibly interesting person all along, but that I had my head too far up my rear end to notice. So true, Christy, so true.

Brad and I started dating soon after that chat with Christy and when I realized there was another girl that could be in the picture. She worked with us, too, and she played golf . . . a guy's dream girl! She was paralyzingly timid, so my extroversion played out well for me. Brad and I were at the Pub and I hinted that if he ever were inclined to ask me out, I would be inclined to say yes. He did and I did–he told me had been waiting patiently for the right moment.

As I wave my fan back and forth to cool my heated brow just thinking about those heated dating days, I wonder, does a woman's sexual history have an impact on her sex life once she's married?

I have a friend who has only ever *"been"* with one guy her whole life, and that is her husband. They have a pretty decent sex life with typical highs and lows. However, I secretly speculate whether she has a sense of regret that she didn't experiment more when she was younger. And then on the other extreme, there are women who would have sex at the drop of a hat when they were dating. Now married, they couldn't be less interested in sex. Why don't they want to have sex with the one person who vowed to love them forever? Perhaps for them, and for other highly sexed daters, it was all part of the chase and dating ritual–once you land a husband, you no longer need that tool. Sex was part of the mating ritual, not part of the marriage ritual. It's amazing how sex before marriage can complicate and lend drama to everyday life, good and bad. Contrast that with sex inside marriage, and if it's going well, it can simplify life, and give you a clear vision of what's going on in your relationship. That's not to say that sex outside marriage is horrible–it can be sexy, and romantic and fun, but it can also cause people to feel lonely and ashamed, and adrift.

As the mother of a young girl, I often worry about how you can convey the complexities of these problems. I know it's incredibly naïve to think we can shield our daughters from embarking on a sexual career too early, but I wish we could. It's not that I'm opposed to sex. Heck, I've been having a ton of it lately and

I've become a real fan–again. And it's not that I'm unaware of the whole hormone thing and how intensely distracting it can be and how the abstinence pledges are really laughable. But for me, it's become screamingly clear that married sex is fundamentally different–and better.

Many a theologian supports the idea that sex and spirituality go hand in hand when you're married, and strangely enough, my Women's Bible Study Group helped my married sex life. I joined this group of neighborhood women several years ago for weekly study sessions. I marveled at the tenacity, smarts, and faith of this group and learned far more than I ever hoped about my faith, my marriage, my relationships, and my life. We've never discussed sex per se, and I'm sure some of the members might blush at the idea that this group of women was the impetus for my embarking on this journey of intimacy. We discuss many of the things that experts tell us are important to marriage–intention, priority, spirituality, forgiveness, and kindness.

My three years with this group of women forced me to dig deeply into what God wants for my life. It was humbling and difficult. But one thing I realized was that part of having a strong marriage meant it was firing on *all* cylinders, and that meant having intimate, deliberate, and meaningful relations with Brad–physically, emotionally, and spiritually. It made me realize that my marriage fuels most everything–our family, our social life, and the overall health and success of our home. I love the idea that for those who practice Judaism, the home is the most sacred place of all–not the temple, not a holy site, but the home. And if you treat the home, and your relationship with the people in it, with the same respect that you would a church or a temple, it would be incredibly difficult to ignore or to overlook them.

So with the thought in mind that the home can and should be a sacred place, it is also a place where the mundane life of marriage happens, too. Sundays are my favorite days to hang out with Brad–spiritually a day of rest. We read the papers together, swap sections, and read articles aloud to each other. We go to lunch after church and then veg out. Most always we have my brother and his family over for Sunday dinner, and we're running around outside playing kick ball or hunkering down in front of a movie. Sundays are generally good days–as a family and a couple.

But all days are not idyllic, and many pass where life is a blur of annoying errands and tasks to do. Simple things can get overlooked, and you'd be amazed at how easy it is to go through your day without really noticing the person with whom you're scheduled to spend the rest of your life. Granted, some people intentionally ignore their spouse but others, like me, simply fall out of touch with them quite by accident.

"Did you get a haircut today?" I asked.

"No, last week," he replied.

"Oh. Well, it looks nice."

"Gee, thanks."

Days are spent as a tag team–meeting the sitter, picking up and dropping off kids, running into the store, picking up dry cleaning. The logistics of today's family are ridiculous–between activities, school, sports, church/synagogue, the house, and so on, it's easy to live a life of coming and going.

I may be overstating the obvious, but daily intimacy with Brad requires me to *notice him.* It regularly prompts me to look him in the eyes and connect in ways–both physical and emotional–that are easily overlooked in the day-to-day machinations of life. Now I have to address him up close and personal, instead of hollering down the hall for him not to forget today is recycling day. Now I physically touch my husband in a different way instead of handing him a dressed child and telling him not to forget the backpack and lunch. And when we're intimate, we are in the moment, and I'm not discussing day-to-day life, because I've learned that multitasking doesn't work in the bedroom. Instead, we're chatting and connecting–you know, couple stuff, the stuff that makes me smile and giggle and feel good about my decision to throw caution to the wind and do it every day. We hug more, we smooch more, we connect more. Because without all the hugging, smooching, cuddling, and yes, sex, it's easy to become a brother and sister act, or a couple of good friends getting together as a family. Brad said to me one day, "You can't have an intimate emotional connection without an intimate physical connection. If you don't connect physically–even if it's just a hug or a kiss–in some way every day, you're just good friends who are raising kids together. And I could probably do that with a lot of people."

Regular intimacy with my husband meant that not every sentence coming out of my mouth started with "could you do [fill in the blank here]." It was a subtle shift, but an important one. And it made me wonder–had I been an accidental poser all these years? Pretending to be in a wonderful and committed marriage that wasn't really all that wonderful as I wasn't committed to regular intimacy with my spouse? I was vowing to fix that now. Which was funny, because unlike my mother, I'm not that handy around the house.

My mother, on the other hand, can fix most anything. Her uncanny way with most things mechanical and all things common sense earned her the nickname "MacGyver." If ever stranded on a deserted island with a fishhook, some rubber bands, and a plunger, you want her there. In fact, once when my parents were in town visiting, I came home from work and collapsed on the couch. "I'm exhausted," I sighed. "What did you two do today?" "Well," my mom replied, "I caulked your shower, fixed your toaster oven, sanded and painted that spot on your front door, and did four loads of laundry. I have a little punch list of things I didn't get to, but I want to review them with you so you can knock them out." I hoped and prayed that I'd inherited just a teeny bit of her MacGyver gene and could find a solution to a problem that at one time I didn't know existed–achieving meaningful intimacy with my spouse.

Brad cannot fix anything around the house. Nothing. He can change lightbulbs, batteries, and trash bags, but that's about it. He can't fix things, tinker with things, or figure out how things work. But with a nudge and a shove and a to-do list, he can get a few things done. He's actually pretty self-motivated when it comes to the kids, and picking up stuff because clutter bugs him far more than it does me. While I am very appreciative that he does it all–don't get me wrong–his puttering around the house is not an automatic turn-on for me as it is for some. For instance, my girlfriend says that she tells her husband that it makes her knees weak when she sees him being all manly with his toolbox fixing things around the house. Upon hearing this, her man is now motoring around the yard in overtime mowing the lawn, repairing leaky faucets, or lifting something heavy and unwieldy. And his little reward at the end of a hard day's housework? A deliciously frisky frolic.

Some friends tell me they get turned on when they see their spouse being a good dad–bonding with the kids, reading them a bedtime story, giving them a bath. They get gaga when their men are being a contributing party to the family unit. But this doesn't do it for me. Brad is an exceedingly attentive dad and kind of gets on my case when *I* don't want to shoot baskets outside or play touch football. But mooning over him playing pickup basketball with the kids? For me, it's part of his D-A-D job description, you know.

What really turns me on these days, and brings back those days of sweaty palms, is when we are in our grown-up lives as married folks, seeing Brad engaged with other *adults.* I like seeing that other people are attracted to him–and *not* in a lusty kind of way but rather that they find him appealing and interesting. This could happen at a dinner party and I see other folks intently listening to him wax on about politics. Or when he tells me about his big presentation to senior management and how much they loved it. Or when he's at a block party throwing his head back and belly laughing at a neighbor's joke.

Those are the times when I am really awestruck by Brad, and it takes the attraction of others to remember why he's so great. Because sometimes I forget–yes, it's awful, but I do forget–that I did, indeed, marry a vibrant, intelligent, handsome, and kind man, and people respond to him as such. What's wonderful and horrible is when you know someone so well that you fail to remember what made him so fabulous to begin with. So often, the gift of familiarity is both a comfort, and a curse.

If Brad knew this, he might not complain as much about our overscheduled social life. I love to see him in the company of others, as the company of me isn't always that fascinating and remarkable–not because I'm not fascinating or unremarkable (because really, I am)–it's just that we know each other *so well* . . . Better, when you have a pulsating social life, you can find out things about your spouse that you might not have known otherwise. For example, it wasn't until a lively game night with friends that I found out Brad had played Jesus in the high school production of *Godspell.* I nearly fell over laughing. I mean, Jesus in *Godspell*–that's not a bit part, might I remind everyone. That was amazing to me. After all, there was a time when I wondered if he believed in Jesus at all.

Later I asked him, "Can you sing?"

"I could then," he replied.

"Do you sing now? Could you serenade me this very minute? On the way home?" I asked, feeling all thirteen-year-old girl to his Donny Osmond.

"Of course not, I don't really sing much anymore. It wasn't that big of a deal."

"Don't sing much? I've been standing next to you in church for years and I've never really heard you sing beyond a murmur. Do you sing in the shower and I've been missing out? Are you a bass or tenor?"

I was bursting with questions–my husband, the singer! Who knew? And yes, I was looking forward to some great theater that night, if you know what I mean. And it took not house-cleaning, not parenting, but game night to get me there.

Back in the La-La Days of Dating, I used to believe there were two kinds of people, people who could marry anyone and be fairly happy, and people like me who were complicated, thorny, and dark, and could marry only one or two people on the planet who "understood" me, and appreciated me for all my tortured complexity. Ha. Ha ha. Ha ha ha. Isn't that rich? Boy, did I have a case of taking myself too seriously or what?

Well, now I believe that there is not one perfect person out there for any given person. Brad is offended by this notion, as we're married and he would like to think that he married the only person for him. But since he was engaged to another before we married, he clearly thought there were two people who would be perfect for him. So he's living proof of my theory.

Me? I am kind of liberated by the notion. You've seen all those old French movies of depressed people aimlessly scouring the streets of Paris looking for the one person in the world who would complete them. Please. The drama! The sadness! The ridiculousness! I now take comfort in the idea that there are lots of people I could have happily married. Because I realize that "love," "true love," "falling in love," and "being in love" are only part of the equation. Am I happy I married Brad? Absolutely. Is he a great fit for me and all my neuroses? Yep. Do I love him? You have no idea how much. Am I in love with him day in and day out of every day? Well . . . it depends. Because here's the deal in Big Boy and Big Girl World: You grow up, you get a job, you pay your bills (on time, mostly). You meet someone who shares common interests and who is attractive to you (and hopefully you are to him). You get along and make sure that you have the same level and kind of dysfunction and want the same things (kids, a houseboat, farm animals). And then you might get married–which means you spend the rest of your lives together. And if you get married, then you have to decide if you want to stay married, because it doesn't just happen. You're choosing a course of action–which is to be and to stay married. And it's easier said than done.

I had a friend who told me that she knew she had married the wrong guy, well, right after she married him. She dated/lived with/was engaged to this man for ten years–that's right, *ten years*–before she finally married him. This epiphany came in Year Eleven and only *after* she had closed the deal. What had changed? What could possibly have been different in Year Eleven that wasn't evident in Years One through Ten? Who knows?

And of course, we all have stories–about our friends or about ourselves–about trying to desperately change a spouse, thinking a relationship would get better, fixing a broken person, or being in love enough to make a romance last. And it still doesn't work. I understand that, too.

So is there such a thing as that Valentine's Day, swoony "true love"–being able to find and love the one person who is absolutely right and perfect for you to the exclusion of all others, who are absolutely wrong and imperfect for you? I don't know. I think people who think they found true love really found a great life partner and built a life that was mutually satisfying and full of wonderful and fond memories. They committed and they compromised and the life they built became their story and *in the end it felt like true love, perhaps.* We're revisionists–it's human nature for the memory to amend history a bit. And in the process, we create love stories, I think. I am thankful to have met Brad, to love him, and to have married him. There is no one else to whom I would want to be married. But is this a love story of historic proportions? Well, time has a role in that. As do I.

So as we celebrate *the most romantic holiday of the year* in the midst of *the most important year of our marriage* (yet), I realize that I am writing a love story with Brad daily. That our story actually started on June 20, 1998. That our life today, tomorrow, and next week is contributing to the story. I can't wait until the kids are older, my work schedule is different, or I lose weight to restart my love story with Brad. Love stories don't happen to you. You create them, you write them, you discover them. And I am responsible for creating one with Brad.

MARCH

Spring Forward, Falling Back

"Honey, are you ready?" Brad called from the den, where he was somehow, through the miraculous powers of his concentration and our DVR system, watching three sporting events at once.

"Almost," I called back. I had enjoyed my beddy-bye glass of milk, rinsed off in the shower, washed my face, brushed and flossed my teeth, plucked my brows a bit (I'm always very busy plucking something), pulled my hair back, applied several coats of very expensive skin stuff, looked in my triple magnifying mirror to see if the expensive skin stuff appeared to be working (not really), tracked down my favorite peppermint lip balm, changed into my pajamas, picked out a book to read, set the alarm, rubbed in some hand lotion, made one final check of my e-mail, turned down the covers, and hopped in.

"Okay, hon, I'm ready. Let's get down to business."

* * *

Brad could score a concerto in the time it sometimes takes me to get ready for bed . . . and ready for him. Since we're scheduling sex these days, I've simply incorporated him into my daily nighttime ritual (or morning ritual, when necessary). And I feel confident that my habitual ritual is driving him nuts. And rightly so, as there was a time when he didn't know all that went on behind the closed doors of personal grooming . . . habits that seem to grow like a Chia Pet as I age. Marriage is many things, but sometimes it's just the naked truth about the real person you've walked down the aisle with.

When Brad and I were dating, he claimed to have a burning desire to learn ballroom dancing. Hey, just like me! And then, poof, after the honeymoon, ballroom dancing was dead to him. Hmmm . . . Eventually Brad learned that my lovely highlights and shiny hair come from a specially calibrated mixture of secret ingredients known only to my hair stylist. And when those courtship foot massages ended, Brad admitted he is grossed out by my feet (I swear there was a time when he told me they were "cute"). And then I finally confessed that I don't care who wins the national football championship . . . horror of horrors.

We've been revealing our true selves bit by bit over the years–from hair dye to two left feet. But a few years ago I did the mother of all baiting and switching–I went from outgoing, fun-loving career gal, to crying, angry, nervous mother-of-two, battling depression. I mean ugly feet are one thing . . .

"Battling depression" sounds overly valiant to me, as I didn't know for a while that I was waging any kind of war on anything. My cheese just slid ever so slowly off my cracker, so that it was barely perceptible at first. "Contracting depression" sounds about right–as I did feel like I was contracting, growing smaller, shrinking, and shriveling up.

I do call it Little D, though, versus Big D, because while Little D was certainly hazardous and a *huge* distraction, it didn't require massive amounts of medication, or hospitalization, and it didn't last years and years, for which I am forever thankful. The weird thing about Little D, though, is her sneakiness. It's like a girl who wants to be friends, sidles up to you, courts you for years and years, and then proceeds to suck all the life out of you until there is nothing left. To quote my dad, "With friends like that, who needs enemies?"

When Little D showed up at the party, it took me by surprise. Little D had been hanging around in the shadows awhile–after the births of both of my children, for example. Of course, hindsight is really "how did you not recognize postpartum when it was knocking you upside the head, girl?" And the winter doldrums (otherwise known as SAD–seasonal affective disorder) had always been a part of my landscape over the years, but it wasn't anything that a sunny trip to Florida or some time in front of those weird sun lamps couldn't conquer.

I thought I had managed to rebuff Little D's overtures–and although my husband would find that statement laughable, I believed it. But one fall, she pursued me with abandon. And in retrospect, I can see how Little D took up residence with me. One of my dearest friends died and was buried on her thirty-seventh birthday.

We knew Christy was going to die. Or rather she had declined to live, in the nicest way possible, of course. That was her way and that is how ALS works. You reach a point where your body has so completely betrayed you that you have to decide: yes or no. Yes, I am okay with how this disease has progressed and I will see it to the end, which means that after my body is unable to move, my lungs will no longer be able to inflate and I will suffocate. Or no, I want more time. And though I still can't move, I will go on a ventilator that inflates my lungs and breathes for me so I won't suffocate and I will buy some days, months, and even years. Christy said yes to the natural course of ALS.

Even when you know someone is going to die, I'm amazed by the capacity to still be shocked by the actual death. The phone call is still startling. The funeral arrangements still seem surreal. The fact that she is gone is astonishing. And apparently, throughout and after all of this, people run into the arms of their loved ones looking for affirmations of life. They need immunity from the tragedy and assurance that it won't happen to them. In the midst of moments of incomprehensible grief or terror, there is apparently this need to physically connect with another human being. Babies conceived around 9/11 are the perfect example, or people who had a lot of uninhibited sex while bombs were raining down on them in the London Blitz in World War II. Dying or the idea of dying creates a craving for connection for things that are, naturally, living. And sexual intimacy is proof that we are very much alive.

But when Christy died, that didn't happen for me.

I mourned alone. I flew solo. I was embarrassed by the floodwaters of grief that spilled over me every day after Christy died. I grieved in the shower, in the car on the way to work, or when washing my face at night. Never in the arms of my spouse, as so many seem to do. I did not seek comfort from Brad–not that it wasn't offered. And I certainly didn't feel an urge to be intimate with Brad–not that it would have been rebuffed. Simply, I was untouched by the idea of touch.

I remember when I got the call. Brad was outside playing with the kids. I opened the front door and stood in the doorway. He turned, almost as if in slow motion. "Christy is gone," I said. It was a cold, hard statement. "Oh, honey, I'm so sorry." But instead of running into his arms, I ran upstairs, closed the bedroom door, and got into bed. I wanted to be alone. Brad came after me, but the door was locked.

I was overwhelmed with life and trying to fit in mourning the death of a friend. It sucked, it really did. My grief was not greater or grander than that of her other friends or her family. There was not the slightest thing remarkable about my grief, save that it belonged to me and that I chose to bear it alone. It was something that was so staggeringly personal that I couldn't share it with anyone. I didn't know how. Not even Brad. It was crushing for us both, yes, but I couldn't do differently.

You see, Christy was so fabulously special that she made you feel that you were her favorite, most fabulously special friend. That seemed to be her job of sorts, to prop up her friends and serve as a reflection of how truly special we all were. Which was ridiculous in a way, as no one was as special as she and we all strived to be even the tiniest reflection of Christy. At least I did. And it seemed I would fail miserably in the year to come.

Not long after Christy's funeral, my dad and career mentor sold his company (which was where I worked, by the way) and retired–a move wholeheartedly supported by our entire family. I was unprepared for how bummed I would be and I missed having him in my corner rooting me on every day at work. I truly mourned the loss of that part of our relationship. But I reasoned I couldn't really be sad because we were all so happy he sold the ad agency and could retire, play fantastic golf, and drive my mom nuts at home.

As though not enough were happening in my life, I thought it would be a good idea if we moved. When you're in the throes of emotional crises, you'd be amazed at the things that seem smart. We were to move, not to a new state or even to a new city, but a mere 1.2 miles from our house–to a wonderful home in a great neighborhood in a great school district where two of my college pals lived.

As soon as we signed the contract for the new house, I freaked. Panic attacks, tears, bursts of anger. It was Charla as Freak Girl. While tears, anger, and panic were part of my repertoire, this was of a new intensity and frequency. I think it was a cumulative freak–all the stuff in my life was catching up to me and I couldn't deal. And by cumulative, I mean having two babies in as many years, finding and hiring a nanny (horrific and comic at the same time), working full-time and later part-time (gratifying and nauseatingly stressful), burying a dear friend, saying good-bye to my dad as day-to-day career coach, and trying to ensure that Brad recognized in me some semblance of the formerly cute, fun, witty, and charming gal he married. I can assure you I failed at that one, in spades–not remotely cute, not at all fun, and all but completely witless. And for some reason, I had really bad hair at the time. Perhaps there is a correlation between my having really bad hair and struggling with Little D? Anyway, Little D was there through all my milestones, patiently waiting in the wings for her official debut.

Fighting Little D off was kind of like those giant roller brushes that you use to blow-dry your hair . . . when you get them all tangled in your hair and you start to panic and yank on the brush, and it just keeps getting worse and worse and worse, and your hair is wrapped every which way around this prickly brush and it hurts like heck but you can't seem to stop tugging. The solution is to be perfectly still and calm and focused. Instead, I was standing there with a giant hairbrush festered into my scalp, sweating and breathless, wondering how the heck I was going to undo this mess.

I would wake up at night, shake Brad awake, and tell him we couldn't move to the new neighborhood "with all those people." I would cry uncontrollably (a common symptom when Little D has you in her grasp), clench his T-shirt in my fist, and wildly look into his face for answers he couldn't possibly give me.

"What people?" he asked. "We know half the people in the new neighborhood."

"Don't be ridiculous, those people don't know us," I hissed. "We have to stay here, we're safe *here*, with these people." The cheese was definitely slipping off the cracker.

My fear of moving was logical, in a way. If you don't know yourself and why you're behaving in such a bizarre way, wouldn't you be freaked out that someone else might find out? I didn't want people who never knew me before to discover how neurotic and weird I was and can be–they might not be thrilled to have me, the cheeseless cracker, as a new neighbor. I could not reason why I would lie awake night after night catatonically staring at the ceiling and wondering if I would ever sleep again. Just like there was no explanation for calling Brad at work and demanding he come home right away to help me find our child's missing shoe.

After several months of me sleepwalking through my life, crying myself to sleep morning, noon, and night, with Brad packing moving boxes every evening after work while I sat in a chair and silently watched him, he politely suggested that I might want to "see someone about this." So I numbly called that little number on my insurance card, and a couple of phone calls later, *voilà*, I was sitting on my therapist's couch letting it all hang out. And according to that newly acquired therapist, I was not good with transitions.

Well, this was good to know, I guess. And while I knew I was a bit neurotic and on occasion compulsive, it had mostly played out okay for me in the past. I disguised all that angst (Little D in her younger, prettier years, I think) with wit, personality, and sheer determination (or so I thought). So yes, knowing that I didn't do well with transition would have been helpful in an earlier chapter of my life, called going to college, when I was shoved out of the proverbial nest and failed to fly.

Cases in point:

Going away to college: Confounding! I couldn't really master that whole getting to class, participating in college life, and conquering the time-management conundrum (until my dad yanked my car and I miraculously made Dean's List to earn it back).

Breaking up with my high school boyfriend: Miserable! I couldn't really get past the idea that the boy I thought I would marry (naïve but true) would dump me unceremoniously after nearly four years for a cheerleader whom he met at a frat party in college. You are not going to believe how I found out he wanted to see other people–my friend Cece had her friend up from NC State for the weekend and brought her by my dorm to meet me. As she surveyed my dorm room adorned with pictures of my adoring boyfriend (who also attended NC State), the friend suddenly left . . . very upset. Apparently her room was adorned with pictures of my adoring boyfriend . . . adoring her. I mean, what are the chances? I was also ill prepared to deal with his comment of "let's still be friends" (also naïve but true) as I thought he meant we would still be friends, which meant I could still call him to hang out. Bad, bad idea, especially when he had new pictures of his adoring girlfriend posted in his dorm room.

Making friends at college: Laughable! Are you kidding me–I could barely get myself to class and get a pen to paper

> to take notes, much less make a friend or two in the dining hall. Which was amazing, really, because I spent a *lot* of time in the dining hall. Note: My mother burst into tears when I walked in the door for Christmas break. I mean, twenty-five pounds . . . what's the big deal?

The only things that saved me at the time were: My parents, who read me the riot act and made me suddenly acquire through sheer osmosis the ability to study, get myself to class, and score decently on my exams. A friend or two who could peer beneath the paralyzing anguish of getting dumped by the boyfriend I was supposed to marry (did I mention he took up with a cheerleader?) and see that I was a fun soul worthy of friendship and attention. My own sheer *chutzpah*, which I am glad to report I still have. And God, who put in my path two little life-altering opportunities that gently nudged (remember, transition = bad) the course of my college career and allowed me to blossom into the slightly caustic, occasionally witty, and fiercely loyal person that I am today. Said person who is prone, of course, to bouts of Little D during times of transition.

So the summer before my sophomore year I broke up with Little D, or we went on hiatus, if you want another way to look at it. I spent the summer studying in Europe, met some terrifically funny and wonderful people, and that fall pledged a sorority filled with women who would impact my life, in a very gentle, nonthreatening way. And the key to those transitions? Good question, friends. I decided, finally, that I was *ready* for them. Yep . . . bring them on.

How did I deal with life's other major transitions?

> I *was* ready for marriage. I'd waited long and hard for Brad to come into my life, and I was delighted to finally have enough sense to recognize the gift that was he. Interestingly, my friend Christy had to give me the nudge on that one, though.
>
> I *was not* ready for kids (although at thirty-one I was not getting any younger and I certainly thought I was ready for kids, at least in theory). In retrospect, I don't know many people who *are* ready for kids, except for my friend Nina. Motherhood was so instinctive and natural to her that we all applied to be adopted by her. In fact, Little D was masquerading as postpartum and how I didn't recognize her is beyond me.
>
> I *was not* remotely prepared to be a full-time working mom, which played out fatefully with Little D coming to check in and see how miserably I was "doing it all." Now, I am not opposed to being a mother "who works full-time outside of the home" and I did just that for a number of years . . . I am merely noting that I was woefully unprepared for it and terribly bad at it.

Not exactly a good track record on the transition front, so I was ready for some tutoring once I realized I was flunking my life so miserably. I'm a smart girl, and to quote Dr. Phil (who is quickly spiraling into Jerry Springer territory, but I am a fan of his early work), "You cannot change what you don't acknowledge." Darn straight.

So after I paid this therapist a buck fifty an hour to tell me I do not manage transitions well, I got home and announced to Brad that (1) he can never leave me; (2) our children can never go to college; (3) we can never move again; (4) my parents are required to live forever; and (5) by the way, did he have any longevity secrets he could pass along posthaste? Oh yeah, and I needed some serious sleep starting this minute and I curled up on the kitchen floor and assumed a sleep position (at least I wanted to). Brad assured me he could only help me with point 1. It was a start.

Later, Brad wanted to know the details. So I told him everything I had learned about myself and this little "situation," including the details on a questionnaire I had filled out at the doctor's office that had covered a variety of issues, including sex. It was the very last question that caused him to pause. The questionnaire read: "How would you answer the following: I am interested in having sex with my partner. (1) Often; (2) Occasionally; (3) Sometimes; (4) Never." Well, you don't have to be a member of Mensa to guess my answer. Brad nodded solemnly when he read it. "We do have a problem," he said. Perhaps seeing in writing that his wife "never" wanted to have sex with him was a shock. Perhaps he had convinced himself that it was really "occasionally" or "sometimes." Either way, I was sad for us both.

That's when I got serious. I sat down with my "transition" therapist and we outlined a game plan. I knew I didn't want to go the medication route, but was willing to try one if the non-pharmaceutical remedies didn't untangle me out of this giant roller brush. Diet . . . good days, bad days. Exercise . . . more times than not, at least in the beginning. Sleep . . . lots and lots of that. Massage therapy . . . heaven on earth. Acupuncture . . . not so much, but hey, I tried. (It was cool at first . . . until my muscles started to twitch and it didn't feel so cool.) Vitamins and supplements . . . some for sleep, others for energy, but who knows if they really worked? And lots and lots of prayer, which proved to be the most important part of this "Little D, be gone with you!" cocktail.

Interestingly, sex wasn't on the prescription list. My therapist brought it up, to her credit. I had scored poorly on sex in that questionnaire, after all. But after I started laughing (or crying, I can't remember) in reference to her discussing the topic, we agreed to table it. I have to admit, though, she was one of the first ever to suggest that although I might have married the World's Most Perfect Man for Charla, it was hardly a perfect union without some semblance of a sex life. At the time, though, it simply wasn't a part of the repertoire for feeling better *for me.* How can you have sex with someone when you feel so sad? How can you want to be intimate when you're waiting to get home so you can cry in the bathroom away from your kids? How in the world can you feel romantic when it's all you can do to get through another day that feels like you're swimming underwater? I mean, people in the movies and in novels seem to run into the intimate arms of a loved one when things get unbearable. Having sex when you're sad, afraid, or overwhelmed should provide comfort, but I never tried it as it was beyond me. I was quietly inconsolable, and I was convinced that having sex wouldn't change that.

Could regular intimacy with a loving spouse have cured me in some way? I wondered. With depression, I believe not. It never occurred to me that sex–or rather intimacy and all that comes with it–could be a management tool for grief . . . or any host of ills. Stress. Anxiety. Pick an angst and test it. "I feel a bad spell coming on, I need to run home to Brad before I fall apart again." It just didn't seem practical. But of course, when you're depressed, your libido is buried somewhere deeper than deep, so at the time, there was no way I could have known.

Fast-forward several years to now, and while Little D is behind me (for now), I realize that there is nothing remotely practical about having sex every day with your spouse either. In fact, as part of this experiment I did indeed learn that if I'm regularly engaged in an intimate relationship with Brad, I really can leverage it to my mental and physical benefit in ways I never considered before (see my back pocket research from January). Back then, I was not aware of the healing benefits of sex with a loving spouse in the confines of a happy, adjusted marriage. But I am now. If you had said to me, "Charla, you should really take up road biking. I think biking twenty to thirty miles a day would really help you feel better/look better/seem better," I would have thought that you were double-dog-down crazy. Ouch, just looking at that tiny seat makes my delicate little arse hurt. But if I was familiar with a bike, I was used to riding it twenty to thirty miles a day, and I had witnessed the many benefits of said activity, then perhaps (1) I would be more apt to believe it, and (2) I would be more apt *to do it.*

We moved to our fab new house in our fab new hood and made some fab new friends–but it took some time. I had to work every day to exorcise Little D a bit more. Oooh, I hated her. I told a few friends about Little D, but not many. Who really wants to know that kind of thing, and quite frankly, up to that point, I thought myself to be made of different stuff. So it was a shock all the way around. Even my best friend, Rita, didn't believe me, and wanted the name and number of my therapist. "You're not the kind of person to get this," she said. "Who did you talk to? I want a second opinion." "Not now," I said. "I'm late for my massage therapy."

So there I was in all my pitiful, depressed glory. Charla–for better or for worse. And there was Brad picking up after me–literally and emotionally. That's when I noticed that, in marriage, you have the little stuff that you think will drive you screaming crazy (like leaving green toothpaste spit sliding down the corner of the sink *every morning*). And then there's the real stuff–like depression, illness, accidents, infertility, unemployment. Once I hit that big-time stuff, it made me realize how small and petty I used to be. Marriage is sometimes about all those crazy left-hand turns during rush-hour traffic on the way to the house–horns blaring, hearts beating, cars swerving . . . and then, finally, peace and safety at home.

APRIL

Spring Training

"This is going to be a huge weekend, honey!" Brad announced on a Friday afternoon.

Great! I'm thinking. What fabulousness has my husband planned for us? What family bonding experience has he thoughtfully conceived and considered? What sweet, quiet romantic moment has he coordinated for the love of his life? I closed my eyes, smiled sweetly, and waited for the inspiring news.

"Well, the Final Four is this weekend and baseball's Opening Day is Monday. The Buckeyes could be playing for a National Championship and the Tribe could be good this year. Whaddya think?"

Well, not much, really.

My husband is a huge sports fan. NBA, NFL, NCAA–you name it. If it's on, he'll watch it. But his true love, besides me? Baseball. Like most baseball purists, he had the game passed down to him. His grandfather played for the Yale Nine. His father was a high school shortstop. His mother cut her baseball teeth on her father's beloved New York Giants and Bobby Thompson's "Shot Heard 'Round the World." The Staten Island Scot's "shot" seared the beauty and legacy of baseball in her mind, which she dutifully passed along to her youngest son. To quote *Field of Dreams* (Brad's all-time favorite movie), "The one constant through all the years has been baseball. America has rolled by like an army of steamrollers. This field, this game, it's a part of our past; it reminds us of all that once was good and could be again."

As a young boy, Brad's love of the game would be forged by his mother shouting and waving her arms in unison with Carlton Fisk as he willed his walk-off home run out of Fenway in the twelfth to send the '75 World Series to Game 7. Reggie Jackson hitting three home runs in Game 6 to seal the Dodgers' fate–and his place in history. Bill Buckner's fateful misplay in Game 6 of the '86 Series. And memories that hit closer to home. David Justice's home run off Jim Poole in Game 6 of the '95 Series to beat his hometown Indians in their first World Series since 1954. And of course, José Mesa's heart-crushing blown save in Game 7 of the '97 Series. To Brad, this is what spring is about. It's about baseball.

I'm up against *this* in the spring, too, friends. That feeling of renewal. That excitement of Opening Day. That "army of steamrollers." That and, of course, the Final Four.

The problem is I am not a huge sports fan, and can't really relate to the mythologizing of sports. On a good day, you could call me a fair-weather supporter of my college football team. I am a tad more passionate about my college basketball team, particularly when they are winning NCAA National Championships, which they do often. But to me, it's just entertainment, it's not life, and it's certainly not obsession.

In fact, when my dad called me in 1995 and suggested that I look into buying some PSLs for the NFL franchise coming to town, I barely blinked.

"What's a PSL?" I asked with the phone wedged on my shoulder as I flipped through files while sitting in my window office on the eighteenth floor of the tallest building in the city. "It's a permanent seat license," my dad said. "It means that you will forever have the rights to buy the tickets for those seats." "Why would I want to do that?" I asked as I spun around and sorted through some other files on the floor in my office. "Well, it's a great investment," my dad patiently answered. "It's a neat way to support your city. You might even enjoy it. And I'll bet there are some guys who would love a gal who has really great seats for the toughest ticket in town." Picture a dangling phone swinging back and forth after being tossed across my desk in a mad rush to get thee to the stadium and pick out those wonderful guy magnets–I mean PSLs. Okay, I wasn't that spastic. But very nearly.

My dad, in a very sweet and appropriate way, has been my wingman over the years. While girls don't traditionally have a wingman, I did–at least in spirit. And while it didn't really help sort through all my dating dilemmas, you've got to admire my dad for trying. For instance, he used to arm my housemate Dana and me with interesting sports stats to offer up when out and about town mixing and mingling with other young singles.

At the time, Dana and I lived together in a small duplex in the heart of Myers Park in Charlotte, within walking distance of our favorite bar. We had three tiny bedrooms and we used the third as a dressing room/closet (it wasn't nearly as glam as it sounds). We would sit on opposite sides of a small table in front of our giant Revlon makeup mirrors plucking, chatting, spraying, and grooming before we finally headed out around 10 P.M. (I know, can you believe we ever went out that late?) Every once in a while we would call my dad and ask for some relevant sports trivia, and we would rehearse in a giggly girly way while sorting through Lancôme lipstick from our free gift with purchase.

Thus prepped, we would head out to the Pub, feeling good, looking cute, and rather bursting with Pertinent Sporting Information. The Pub was in a converted house in a historic neighborhood. It was dark and smoky and intimate, with a fireplace in one corner, a bar in the other, and oddly mismatched tables and chairs. There were several televisions posted around the bar (tuned to the sports event *du jour*), and in warm weather, they opened a giant brick patio. The Pub served the requisite bar food and lots of ice-cold buckets of beer. It was homey and local and one of our hangouts at which to mingle and pretend to watch sports.

One evening, we were one beer into masquerading as Scintillating Sports Enthusiasts, and before I could even wipe the froth off my lip, bam–it was over. That's right, just like that: Dana had fired off all our collective sports ammunition before she was done with her first Miller Lite. There was not one bullet left in our arsenal about college hoops, the NBA, or how any decent second baseman has to hit better than .315. Nada. I was stunned! I looked around to see if anyone else had noticed. And Dana just stood there beaming in all her Scintillating Sports Enthusiast glory.

I couldn't possibly be mad; I was too busy being surprised. My sweet little roomie, Dana, who was so soft-spoken and kind and not remotely competitive. Well, well, still waters run deep, don't they? I am not suggesting that she was not soft-spoken, kind, or even competitive, but rather my girl knew to seize the moment and so she did. The things you can do when you have a wingman. It's a powerful feeling, as Dana will tell you.

Dana eventually did meet her future husband at a "My Dad as Wingman" expedition, but it was not at a bar. Thanks to Dad, we had enviable seats at a great three-day college basketball tournament crawling with cute eligible postgrads. Chris sat behind us throwing popcorn in Dana's hair (is that guy smooth, or what?) and the rest is history. Now Dr. Phil advises single women to meet guys in a content-rich environment (i.e., sporting venues), and gets highly compensated for it. But my dad knew that years ago, and it did prove out for Dana and Chris. I should really pay my dad for all this great advice.

I know that my friend Julia is cringing right now as she reads this. She comes by all her sports gravitas the good old-fashioned way–she earns it. She is a huge sports fan, fanatically tracks sports stats, and would be so disappointed by our sports plagiarism. But hey, a girl's gotta do what a girl's gotta do. Because in the midst of finding someone else, don't we sometimes pretend we're something we're not? It inevitably doesn't work, mind you, in the short run or long term, but we're all just scouting, whether it be innocent, or not so innocent. So Dana and I, while we do love a good Super Bowl party or a Sunday tailgate, are not sports fans at heart.

Neither is my friend Allison, who managed to camouflage for a long while that she did not share her husband's fanatical and all-consuming passion for Auburn football. In fact, she was not interested in football, period. She and her husband were at the Auburn/Georgia football game. It was the fourth overtime, 30 flipping degrees, and the crowd was going wild. This game was going down in the history books of football as the stuff of legend, and Allison's husband looked over at her, the woman with whom he'd chosen to share his love and his interests, and *she was checking her watch.* "Up until that time, I had kept hidden my sheer disinterest in football, except as it might pertain to tailgating, what one might wear to the game, or who one might see at the game. But I was totally outed."

Standing in freezing temperatures as my team went into overtime became a new pastime; I did end up securing those four lower-level, end-zone PSLs (which did turn me from a Pathetic Sports Loser into a Popular Sports Lover for at least eight weekends a year). And I became a very popular girl. It also proved to be a major bonus when Brad and I started dating.

In fact, Brad claims those four little PSLs were a deal maker for him. "I mean, you came to the table with a dowry, for Pete's sake!" he once claimed. "It was awesome."

"Are you telling me you married me for my lifetime tickets to the NFL?" I screamed. I was incredulous.

"Of course not," he said. "But it was a nice perk. Kind of like watching the Final Four when your favorite team is in it! You're going to watch anyway–but now it's a lot more exciting!" Alrighty then.

But I guess that's appropriate since most men eat, live, and breathe sports. If they're not watching sports–they're watching sports movies. Men who do not weep at the miracle of their first child being brought into the world will cry like babies when Ray Kinsella "has a catch" with his dad in *Field of Dreams*. My husband becomes a blubbering fool every time it's on. There are movies he could watch over and over no matter when and where he's tuning in. There's *Hoosiers*–what guy, he claims, doesn't get choked up when they run "the picket fence" and Jimmy Chitwood hits the game winner? Football? Look no further than *Brian's Song*. If you're a man and you don't come unglued during the final scene when Billy Dee Williams's Gale Sayers comes to the hospital as James Caan's Brad Piccolo is taking his last breath, then, according to Brad, you don't have a soul.

Now that Brad is no longer pretending to be interested in taking ballroom dance with me, he is either watching sports–or a movie about sports–or tracking sports online. In the old days before we got married, Brad was so wrapped up in the success of his three favorite teams that the core of his very happiness was deeply invested in wins and losses. He would be moody, quiet, and cranky if his teams lost. He would skulk around the house, muttering under his breath or calling his best friend to vent and scream. Before we met there were days where a particularly painful loss could keep him at home all day, unshaven and in a funk. Brad's old roommate claims he used to root for the Browns even though he was a Bears fan because Brad would "be insufferable at least through Wednesday."

If his teams won, Brad would be ebullient, happy, and carefree. The world just seemed brighter to him. He would want to celebrate, to study every sportscast as they fawned over his team's victories, and to cruise the Internet to find glowing updates and to memorize stats. I mean, the energy and emotion Brad expended to follow not one, but three or even five, sports teams could fuel a small third-world country. Just imagine if he spent all that energy and emotion on me, it would be . . . well, it would probably be incredibly claustrophobic and cloying, so never mind that point.

My real point is before he had a wife and kids and a mortgage, Brad held sports in the center of what most women would consider a small, unhappy, and slightly pathetic life. A life for which most men probably pine and reminisce. Today, Brad works hard to keep his sports mania in check–he probably does a lot of his obsessing when I'm not around. But either way, today there is a discernible difference in the grip that sports has on his life. What's the diff? Well, not to beat a dead horse, but we do have that DVR, and a couple of growing kids who need his attention, and a wife who is trying to connect with him. All this encourages a good deal of personal growth, don't you think?

So today, we don't fight over the remote, and we don't keep score of who got to watch what last. And we never argue over what's more important–some meaningless baseball game or who gets voted off a reality show. This does not mean that we are saints and never argue, but it's primarily because we have a lot of televisions in our house (including one in the bedroom), and peace is kept simply by going to another room. Also, we've both realized that we have to keep our television viewing in check and under control, and to throw some hissy fit about the television would just be one giant step back. In our current house, the television sits at a funny angle in the bedroom and you can't change channels with the remote without sitting up and leaning out of the bed with your arm stretched out and around like a coat hanger antenna. It's simply too much work for me to watch television in bed, if you can believe it.

Brad and I have never been marital scorekeepers. This is due to several reasons. The first is that I have a terrible memory and my ability to track what Brad has and has not done required massive brainpower that has slowly oozed from my ears since the birth of my children. The second is that we have those handy job descriptions.

In fact, now that we're on the same team, so to speak, and aspiring to all things intimate, there is no need. I no longer have to note in the back of my head, "Well, I guess I'll have to give it up this weekend since it's been a while." And Brad no longer has to count back the days or even weeks to locate the fading and distant memory of us rolling in the hay. Yes, the only things I'm counting are the days until this sex every day thing is over.

While I am still committed to the overall arrangements, I must admit that the day-to-day mechanics are getting a tad bit old.

But sex should be a team sport, and I am indeed a member of Team Muller. Obviously, having sex alone is not as fun. But the more salient point is that Brad and I now have to work together to make sex work. A concept that, until now, was sadly foreign to me. It turns on its head the adversarial power play between spouses–men gaming on how to get it, and women gaming on how to get out of it. What if, gasp, Brad and I aspired to the same things sexually *for the rest of our lives*? Without even knowing it, our sex-every-day arrangement made us teammates. Would it stick? I wondered. Because to paraphrase Yogi Berra, from a woman's perspective, sex is 90 percent mental and the other half is physical. (He also famously said, "It ain't over 'til it's over"–but that's a reference for another chapter.) For men, I'd have to deduce that sex is 100 percent physical, and if there is a nice emotional connection, that's just gravy.

I've referenced sportsmanship and this is a good time to address the critical role that it plays in this intimacy-every-day arrangement. And while I've done my best to conduct myself in an appropriate manner behind closed doors, I'm amazed that this agreement has forced me to be a stellar player on and *off* the court. I am finding I must treat my teammate with respect, encourage him with a "good game" even when he didn't (if you get my drift), conduct myself with integrity, and abide by the rules with a good and fair attitude. It's not been impossible, but it has forced a kind of mindfulness.

For the most part, though, I've always considered myself a

good sport. Like the time I ran against Roger Brown for Student Council. I voted for him in a terribly misguided gesture of goodwill and sportsmanship and he voted for . . . himself. You know where this is going–Roger Brown won . . . by *one vote*! "You don't deserve to win if you're not willing to vote for yourself. How stupid," he commented. Actually, I thought our votes would cancel out each other (like Brad and I often do when we vote on local bond issues), but it really was a stupid gesture of sportsmanship on my part that nearly ended my Student Council career.

Sportsmanship aside, Brad and most men struggle to keep their sports obsessions in check. Brad has to restrain himself from checking on his fantasy baseball team or the odds for the latest Ohio State game. Likewise, women have to keep their ex-man obsessions in check. Too much energy is spent on thinking, "I wonder what [INSERT NAME HERE] is doing right now?"

Thomas Wolfe said you can't go home again. Which is funny, because he and I share the same hometown and I go home a lot. Arguably, when he wrote that incredibly controversial, thinly veiled memoir that alienated everyone close to him, I would think it was indeed awkward to go home again. For me, I am happy and grateful to go home and always try to be nice to everyone there so that I am welcomed home again and again. But sometimes going home again is still awkward. First off, because you have friends there who never left. Or you have friends there who aren't really your friends anymore and you feel awkward running into them. Or you decide it's a good idea to call your ex-boyfriend from high school to see if he's coming to your twentieth high school reunion.

I know, I can't believe it either.

I went home to visit my parents and scheduled to meet my oldest friend, Marcie, for a drink. I worked my entire day to accommodate this evening out with her. I wore out the kids at the pool. I fed them early and I transitioned them to Brad so that I had enough time to take a leisurely shower and blow out my hair. I left the house and was off to meet Marcie at The Usual Suspects, a local bar on the other side of town. It was summer in the mountains and the weather was so gorgeous it deserved a special name, like breezi-abulous or something. I was relaxed, free, and clean–feelings that were hard to come by in those days. I was listening to the Eagles, basking in a peaceful, easy feeling.

I drove past my high school–a proud, impressive stone building that sits regally on a hill. I remembered my high school career–friends, beach trips, teachers, and of course, Alex, a high school boyfriend. We had a bad breakup–primarily because I thought I would marry Alex and he did not think he would marry me. Not exactly on the same page, the two of us. He was a nice guy, and as far as high school beaus are concerned, I did okay. "Hmmm," I found myself thinking, "I wonder what he's doing now . . ." So I decided to find out. I called Information, and before I knew it, Information had connected me to Alex's home phone, and that phone was ringing.

This is a good time for me to share a few bits of advice for those folks who decide out of the blue to call an old boyfriend from high school. The first and most critical piece of advice is this: *Don't do it!* Forget about closure. Forget about fond memories. Forget about that lame excuse that he really cared about you and you want to know how he's doing. Forget that you are freshly bathed, driving across town with the windows down and feeling great. Just put down the phone and walk (or drive) away and meet your friends. It's just not going to go well. I promise.

I didn't call for closure. I had gotten that many years back when Alex had called to "check in" and hinted at a possible reunion. "Are you kidding me?" I screamed into the phone. "Really! After you totally hosed me for a college cheerleader and stomped all over me and left me for dead, now you want to check in?" I was lathered up, I mean this breakup was a major emotional setback that I was still recovering from. "Listen, Alex," I fired into the phone. "I don't want you to ever call me again. In fact, I don't want you to ever ask my friends about me or even think about me–do you understand? We are so done." There was a long pause.

"Well, you don't have to be such a bitch about it," he finally said and hung up. That was some serious closure, girls. So in a way, I guess it was my turn to "reach out."

If, however, you choose to ignore my first line of advice, please work through a few key elements before you dial.

1. What exactly are you going to *say* that doesn't make you sound like a pathetic idiot?

2. If the call goes to voice mail, what exactly will you *do* that doesn't make you seem like a pathetic idiot?

3. If you choose to leave a message–again, what will you say that doesn't make you sound . . . well, you get the idea.

You'd be right if you guessed that I was totally unprepared to address any of these questions. One of the curses of twenty-first-century technology is that it is nearly impossible to stalk and/or hang up on people without being found out or being terrified that you will be found out. So I was stuck.

"Hello?" a small, reedy voice asked.

Oh, crap. Critical Element No. 4: What will you do if someone other than your ex answers the phone? Oh, the clumsiness of it all.

"Um, hi, is your dad there?"

"You mean Daddy? Uh-huh, hang on."

"Ddddaaaaaaaadddddddy. Telephooooooone."

Wow, now everything was moving in slow motion. And it dawned on me as I cruised across town with the wind blowing in my hair that this was a royally bad idea. I won't even bore you with the details except to say that it took Alex forever to get to the phone because he was on his business line when I called, and when he picked up my call, he asked if he could call me right me back. And then I said no and he insisted yes and then I said no and we had this uncomfortable back-and-forth exchange until the caller on his other line actually hung up on him and suddenly he had all the time in the world. As if things could get any more awkward. I managed to find out that he worked in technology (I think that's what he said) and was married (that I'm sure of) with three sons (or maybe daughters), including a set of twins (from what I can recall). But this is what I did remember–he was not going to our twentieth high school reunion because (and I'm paraphrasing) "I got so knee-walking drunk at our tenth reunion I'm not sure anyone will talk to me this time around. I was hungover for days. Hell, it was awful."

Well, there you have it.

I gave him a quick update on me (as if he really wanted to know), wished him well, hung up, and pressed down on the accelerator. I sat up straight in my seat, shaking my head as if to get rid of the mental picture of a slightly balding guy knee-walking drunk at our reunion and his wife having to lug him into a car. As I pulled into the parking lot of the bar, I realized I was sweating. So much for that peaceful easy feeling.

Marcie and her friends could not *believe* I called him. Marcie, my friend since practically birth, was impressed. "That took a lot of guts, sweetie. I'm proud of you–you should feel empowered."

"Are you kidding me?" I said. "It was the most gawky, discombobulating thing I have brought upon myself in a long time. Can I still be a dork at thirty-nine? What was I thinking?"

Well, clearly, I still wasn't thinking when I got home because I couldn't wait to repeat the tale of my awkward phone encounter with Alex. My brother and mother were appalled. "You did that?" My dad laughed out loud–"Good for you, how is old Alex anyway?" My sister-in-law was indifferent–"Who's Alex?" But here's the kicker: Brad was peeved–"Why would you ever want to call an old boyfriend?" And really, I had no idea. For Brad, it's like watching José Mesa's blown save again. Why would he want to relive that kind of thing?

"I mean, what were you thinking when you decided to call Alex?" Brad asked me later that night as we were getting ready for bed.

"Clearly, hon, I wasn't thinking. Which is what makes the story so funny and painful."

"Well, I don't find it funny, I think it's weird that you would want to call Alex after all these years. Would you approve of me calling an old flame?"

Well, it would depend. There is a big difference in my book between a high school girlfriend and a former fiancée. High school was, sadly, dog years ago . . . but a fiancée? Well, that was practically yesterday. So the same rules just don't apply. I guess I could probe deep, deep inside my psyche and come up with some explanation for why on that beautiful day I felt the need to call my high school boyfriend. But I don't think there is any explanation. I think, for once, it is what it is. "Well, there's nothing really to it," I answered. "And if there were anything to it, I wouldn't have shared it with the world and I certainly wouldn't have told you."

He studied that point for a while. And I studied him. I was really intrigued by the fact that he was bothered–okay, maybe even jealous–that I called my old high school boyfriend. I mean, Brad Muller is pretty great and so much more than I deserve day in and day out (except when he refuses to eat breakfast for dinner) that to compare him with Alex is very nearly impossible. So on the one hand, it made me feel good. But on the other hand, it felt so, well, "high school," almost silly and very unnecessary. Like when Marcie and her boyfriend would pick me up for high school in his white Camaro with AC/DC blasting so loud that I had a viselike headache *before* AP English with Mrs. Reinhardt (it was usually the other way around). If there was some emotion other than nosiness embedded in this gesture, then I am not self-aware enough to know what it is. So instead I just pinned it all on Brad and his stuff, which was silly, unnecessary, and very "high school" on my part.

So then I asked some girlfriends about it, and while I find this terribly hard to admit, they disagreed with me. "Just because you don't care about an old boyfriend doesn't mean you don't *care* about an old boyfriend." Well, that was a bit cryptic. "Why did you call him? Why didn't you just Google him?" Apparently, Googling old boyfriends is practically an art so I dropped everything and immediately Googled Alex (as I suspected, nothing to note on the World Wide Web). Another asked why I didn't coordinate a "run-in" with him so I could check him out in person. As my girlfriend noted, "I ran into a Top Five All-Time Crush the other day and I thought, "Damn, he's still cute after twenty years." I don't know why I didn't do a run-in.

And before I pull out all that psychobabble about how our pasts craft who we are today and blah, blah, blah, the long and short of it is this: Sometimes you just want to know. Sometimes you're just driving across town, listening to the Eagles and waxing nostalgic about a nice time in your life, and you just want to know how someone is doing. There is no ulterior motive or current flaw in your life other than the fact that you're human and you just want to know. And of course, there is no wrong in that. Certainly you can't divorce yourself from your past but it doesn't mean you regret the present. I suppose I could have Googled Alex (less embarrassing) or coordinated a "run-in" with him (more work) or simply let the moment pass without action (definitely my best bet). And perhaps I would have felt differently had I discovered that Alex was living some over-the-top life. But in reality, he wasn't. And if I had to say who had fared better after we "moved on," I would have to say me (and that has nothing to do with anything except my own hubris).

Later I would tell Brad: "Honey, I don't know why we're even talking about this. But here is one thing I can tell you for sure–Alex is *not* having sex every day with *moi. You are.*" It's not like I was keeping Alex in the bullpen in case I needed to call him up later. No, we were a bad fit the first time around.

Nice save, Charla. Batter up!

I do have a friend who told me that if anything happened to Hubby No. 1, she has someone waiting in said bullpen. Now I haven't quizzed her at length on this second-string guy, but I do know that he's pals with her current husband, if that doesn't beat all. And in reality, this probably happens more than we'd like to admit. My mother always kiddingly claimed the only man for whom she would leave my father was Robert Urich. Remember him? He was in *Vega$* (I love that *$*) and *Spenser for Hire*. Unfortunately, he died in 2002, which was terribly sad for my mother and probably not so much for my dad, who surely had grown tired of her swooning.

Who hasn't thought, at the end of a really bad argument with her husband, what life would be like if only she had married the one who got away–especially a good-looking guy like Robert Urich? Who hasn't sat at the computer at work, taking a break from writing up that report, and Googled her ex-boyfriend (apparently every woman in America but me). While there is something seemingly uncomfortable about this strategy, you do hear of many men whose wives have been suffering for years from cancer, and when these poor women finally pass, the widowed men are dating again within months. While this may appear shocking and upsetting, the reality of living with death for years probably made the surviving spouse want to get back in the game, and quickly.

But sometimes that relief pitcher can be worse than the starter–I mean, they are a "backup" after all. One friend's sister got divorced, and she looked up an old boyfriend. This is the man she'd been dreaming of–they had a really passionate relationship with fights, and drama. And he was single, and they did get back together. After a couple of weekends away together, she thought, "What on earth was I thinking?" It had been that perfect romance in her memory when she was unhappy with her husband. She was sorely disappointed when she met up again with the real deal.

Perhaps people break up and make a trade because they think that it's going to be better with this guy, and the grass is greener. Sure, marriages break up for lots of tragically sound reasons: infidelity, abuse, the list can go on. But to kick out the starter because you're bored with him, or because he's not scoring well, that's just unfair. As a friend of mine noted on her second marriage: "I compare and contrast my first husband with my second husband all the time. Then I finally figured out the common denominator is me."

I think both Brad and I would be devastated if we found out that the other had somebody, at least mentally, warming up for us in the bullpen. However, I do think if either one of us died, we both would like the other to remarry . . . But on the one hand, my friend does have a point and I'm paraphrasing when she says, "If my husband dumped me for a bench player, it had better be someone not remotely like me. Because if he dumped me to marry a better version of me? Well, I would be really pissed off. And besides, everyone backslides, so he'd really be marrying me all over again. So why make the trade?"

On an alternate tack, one of my friends says she's not interested in remarrying should the worst happen to her marriage. But she does have someone in the bullpen, only it's not a man. She would move in with a woman, and no, she's not a lesbian. She just thinks everyone needs a wife . . . even women. "I would live in a house with a female roommate who would do her share of the cooking, cleaning, and maintenance," she commented. "Wouldn't you miss being married?" I asked. "Nah, you can always date. And then come home to a nice, clean, and well-organized house." It does sound pretty good, doesn't it? I guess that's what you call a free agent.

While we're all dreaming of a world where men reject sports and instead favor a good Lifetime movie and a glass of chilled chardonnay, I recognize that this is never going to happen in my galaxy. Instead, Brad and I cozy up with some Bud Lights to watch some major sports drama unfold in Technicolor. While I may take breaks to read my book, thumb through a cooking magazine, or fold some laundry, we're there together. And if his teams lose, no worries. We're on to our game of doubles . . .

MAY

May Flowers . . . I Mean Showers

"Okay, honey," I said as I came out of the bathroom, pulling my hair into a ponytail. My teeth were brushed and my face was freshly scrubbed. "You ready?"

"You know, sweetie, I think I'm going to take a pass tonight, if you don't mind," Brad said, hidden from view behind the pages of Newsweek.

My hands stopped in midair, and I very slowly turned around. "I'm sorry, but could you repeat that? I thought I heard you say you were going to take a pass."

He peeked around the magazine. "I am. I'm tired, and I have a big meeting tomorrow, and we've been having a lot of sex lately."

As if I hadn't noticed.

The children are almost done with school. The garden is ablaze with blooming azaleas, and the crepe myrtles are getting ready to show. It's now eleven months into this year of daily intimacy. I'm feeling like I'm running a marathon and getting agonizingly close to the finish line. I go through moments of elation–a real endorphin rush that I have been able to make good on this gift to Brad. And then there are moments where I've hit the proverbial wall, and feel like beating myself over the head with the nearest flat iron or maybe a spatula.

While I have mixed emotions about what we've done, Brad's emotions have been pretty consistent–utter and sheer delight. It's not until spring that he's even exercised his right to take a pass (well, there was that New Year's Eve thing). To me, that's an amazingly long stretch of time, and it's likely that if Brad had offered me this birthday present and it was Day 305, I would have "passed" on the offer about 200 times now already, give or take a dozen. Ten months into this offering and the difference between the sexes when it comes to sex couldn't be more evident. It was an "aha" moment. I was beginning to suspect that men and women were so totally on opposite ends of the sex continuum that men would always take the opportunity to have sex, and women, after the first three years of a relationship, would try to avoid sex. It was comforting to know that after a certain period of satiety, and exhaustion, Brad could admit that he didn't need to have a "go" that night. Across the huge gulf of sex drive, a bridge had been built.

My girlfriends agree that men are so differently wired from women in this regard that we will never know what it is like to have that kind of drive. One friend, the mother of three children under the age of five, said, "My husband knows he's a frisky dog, and I'm not. I don't want to all the times he does–which is all the time. While sex is important to me intellectually and it's really important to my marriage, it's harder to turn on to it. He knows not to feel rejected because he knows I'm not wired like him."

But a lot of men do feel rejected, my husband included. It wasn't until this daily gift that Brad finally admitted that my dubious dodging–while not an outright "no" to sex–still stung. "I know you're avoiding sex and it bums me out," he later told me. "It's humiliating to have to barter or game for sex. Why can't you want it as much as I do? I'm your husband, for Pete's sake, not some cheesy college guy looking to get lucky."

My best friend, who has never struggled with her weight, sometimes "forgets to eat." She is energetic, athletic, a driving Type A who is always on the go–running errands, running a marathon, or running her three kids somewhere. Now I'm sorry, you can forget to pick up the dry cleaning, or forget that it's "Pajama Day" at your daughter's school, or that you had a 7:30 A.M. staff meeting that you slept through. But forget to eat? Never for me. But she is tall and thin and I'm, well, not–so maybe she has a point. I take such pleasure in food, in taking a meal, in cooking and preparing a meal, and in all things gastronomical, that "forgetting to eat" is very nearly impossible for me. I mean, God intended for us to eat–that is what fuels our body. And apparently, He also designed sex for that whole procreation thing. So yes, I will never miss a meal. And no, sex doesn't have the same urgency for me as feeding my hunger. But I wonder, is that how it works for men? Do men take such pleasure in sex, in taking sex, in thinking about and preparing for sex, that "forgetting to have sex" is very nearly impossible for them? Perhaps if I likened having sex with my pleasure in food, I could for a tiny moment–albeit very tiny–appreciate where Brad is coming from. Or maybe not.

The sex drive discrepancy causes many women to do a lot of subtle dodging. I present Exhibit A: Charla Muller prior to July third. One woman I know stays up until midnight so her husband will be fast asleep when she tiptoes in for bed. Another friend told me, "My husband wants me to go to bed at the same time, because he doesn't want me to wake him up when I come to bed, and he always wants to think there might be some lovin' on tap. I always take longer in the bathroom. And I found out by accident that he often will fall asleep while I'm still in the bathroom. Now I might take a little longer flossing my teeth, and applying moisturizer, to get out of having sex."

But those hubbies still give it the old college try. My friend Wendy told me at a cocktail party, "If I don't have sex with him, he's going to start *rubbing* my back and *rubbing* my back, and pretty soon there's going to be a hole in my back, because he is just *not* going to stop trying. The very few times that I have said no, it's become a bit competitive and I know he'll just come right back at me the next night." I asked Wendy what she did when he kept trying to have a romp with her. "Who was that woman, was it Dr. Ruth?, who said, 'How hard is it to give just two minutes, just two to five minutes, for the life of your marriage?' So I'll be like: 'Okay, let's just do this, it'll be a relief for you, and then we can just go to bed, and I won't be lying there with you rubbing a hole in my back.'"

My sister-in-law, the investment banker, has a more pragmatic approach to intimacy. Like any good business school graduate, she compares intimacy to the concept of the time value of money. The idea is that a dollar today is worth more than a dollar tomorrow, because of the beauty of compound interest. So if we invest a dollar today, we make interest on it, and then make interest on the interest, and that dollar will be worth much more than a dollar saved next year. She has brilliantly correlated this idea with time value of intimacy. Namely that having sex today is always worth more than having sex tomorrow. We reap the benefits of having sex plus all the goodwill it generates for our marriage and in the eyes of our spouse. In turn, this accrues (like compound intimacy interest) and we now have a "bank account" of intimacy that can be reflected in less stress between partners, less anxiety, a closer relationship, and so on. An added kicker is the assumption that sex today is going to be better than sex tomorrow . . . and God forbid, if there's ever an accident, you know?

And as I mentioned earlier, there is no better time than the present to hop into some good old-fashioned intimacy, because none of us are getting any younger and we should go ahead and carpe diem. But the correlation to money does have a flaw. Unlike the financial world, where you can invest a big chunk of change early in the game and reap the rewards, I have learned the hard way that I have to continually make deposits into my intimacy account to keep it earning anything. I can't have a ton of sex in January and then expect it to sustain Brad until Memorial Day. The more deposits, the better, for sure. But the deposits need to be regular and thoughtfully timed to really experience any payoff. So it seems I'll get the best bang for my buck (I know, I'm giggling, too) if I invest early and often, and just plain make it a habit.

I'm not alone in having to manage this sexual dichotomy. Many of my friends agree with me that, for the most part, women don't have the same sexual frequency preferences as our spouses, and we have to work to make deposits into the bank of intimacy. One exception to the rule is my friend Sofia, who has always matched–or possibly exceeded–her spouse in terms of sexual appetite. In fact, when she and her husband married, they signed a Life Agreement, which I think is similar to a prenup, only it's not valid in a court of law (to which I say, then why do it?). Anyway, this Life Agreement outlined that each expected a fair amount of intimacy . . . or else. Or else what? I asked, dying to know. "Well, one of us can call the other to 'council' and they are required to address the 'we didn't have sex last night, so whassup with that?' question." And then what, I wonder . . . a flogging with wet noodles?

So we can all say we want it, we can all agree "intellectually," as my friend says, that it's the right thing to do, and we can still bob and weave around having it. But the age-old problem still exists in this modern twenty-first century: How do you manage expectations, needs, rejections, and disappointments without making yourself and your partner miserable, or filing for divorce, or contemplating an affair? With Brad and me, we finally discovered what Sofia has probably known all along–discussing sex, keeping it on the radar, and making it a priority are all worthy endeavors.

When I was twenty, I embarked on a different endeavor. I moved to New York City for the summer. I was in love with the city before I arrived. I loved her from afar, kind of like how I loved Parker Stevenson from afar during his *Hardy Boys* years. I had visited the city twice, including once with my parents. The trip with my parents was a high school graduation gift. I bought a Louis Vuitton handbag at Saks Fifth Avenue, and I thought I would die from the thrill of it all. While I saw the typical parts of Manhattan during that short forty-eight hours, there was nothing I saw that I didn't love. Who wouldn't want to live in a city with so much energy and action? She had put her best foot forward during my visit, and I was desperate to return.

So I did. I went to live in Manhattan the summer before my senior year of college. My home that summer was in NYU medical student housing. The apartment was a two-bedroom efficiency that I sublet from the nephew of a business associate of my father's. I had a grossly underpaid internship at a PR agency that had nothing to do with NYU or medical students, but I found the place quickly, and it was cheap. Accompanying me to New York were two suitcases of clothes, my dad's worn blanket from college (emblazoned with a university crest), and my hair dryer. One bedroom was crammed full of stuff and the other bedroom had a single bed and a desk. Later, I would close the door to the second bedroom because I had seen mice and had no device to manage them other than to slam the door and shove several towels at the bottom. I was hoping to starve them, or send them to another equally seedy neighboring apartment. The second day I was there, I claimed a small television set from the garbage room in the building.

Fortunately, I had a very genial and helpful cabbie from the airport, who gave me a much-needed lesson in New York geography. He told me that Manhattan is eight miles long and two miles wide. Fifth Avenue bisects the city so all streets west are labeled West and all streets east of Fifth Avenue are labeled East. All street numbers emanate from magical Fifth. That means that 40 West Fifty-seventh Street is close to Fifth Avenue. Don't go past Ninety-eighth Street on either side (this was 1988, remember). If you can, take the bus instead of the subway. It's simply more pleasant. That advice, and a few hundred-dollar bills from my dad, was all I had going for me.

I knew no one in New York except one girl from college, who was a year older and fully employed. Actually, there was another girl I knew from Long Island who would be a college roommate the following fall semester. But since my geography of New York was laughably poor, I had no idea she was so close. For all I knew, Long Island was near Syracuse. So I never called her and missed a grand opportunity to know *two* people in the greater New York City area that summer. I was quite embarrassed and sad on move-in day that fall when I discovered that a real friend had been only a forty-minute train ride away. But I digress. I did keep calling the older girl who had already settled into the city. She could not have been less interested, but I kept calling her and calling her before I arrived and she must have noted the desperation in my voice because, finally–finally!–I snagged an invite to go out with her my first weekend in the city. Great, only ten more weekends for me to fill.

Our outing was a party on the Upper West Side. I barely knew where the Upper West Side was, but I was thrilled. I could have cared less how or if I was going to fit into what I thought was a hip New York City party scene, I was just desperate for the company, even the company of six snooty investment bank trainees, also newbies to the New York City party scene. So there I was, slightly out of place but beaming from ear to ear, thrilled to be traveling in a pack of young urban professionals. I was twenty years old.

After arriving at my friend's apartment, we met up with her other friends and started out on foot. It was a pretty June night, the kind of night that makes you pause and really appreciate that everything is perfect–the temperature, the air–not too hot, not too cold–just right. We turned the corner onto West Eighty-fourth Street looking for the walk-up with the purported party, when suddenly the guy walking in front of me grabbed his ankle. "Crap, something hit me in the ankle." We all bent over for inspection and heard a ping here and a ping there. Metal bouncing off concrete. A cracked windowpane. It took only a second (or perhaps two, as we had had some cocktails) to realize that someone was *shooting* at something–or us.

Before I could think about the novelty (or horror, depending on how you look at it) of being in New York City in the middle of gunfire, I was hit in the face. I grabbed my right cheek and my eyes stung with tears. I turned away in pain. Crap, I couldn't cry in front of six snooty investment bank trainees whom I hardly knew!

I crouched over and held my breath as I examined the wound. Well, at least it didn't go all the way through, I thought to myself. Isn't the twenty-year-old mind an amazing thing? Had I been my current forty-year-old self, I would have been absolutely freaking out and waiting for another bullet to pierce my carotid artery and bleed out right there on West Eighty-Fourth Street. But no, my twenty-year-old self was still standing, possibly in the line of fire, looking on the bright side of things and thanking her lucky stars that the bullet didn't go *all the way through.*

The group huddled around me with enough concern to make me feel a bit better. Once they were comfortable that I wasn't going to die, they stayed on course, not to be deterred by a little ole thing like a *bullet.* My friend, who had a rare moment of decency, waved them ahead and took me to nearest deli for a look-see.

We walked a few blocks past the neon lights of a dry cleaner, a pizzeria, a Tasti D-Lite, Pinky Nail, and several bars. My friend pulled me into the deli, where fluorescent lights cast a weird green light on everything. "Let me see," she said.

I pulled my hand away and blood was everywhere. The owner of the deli, a small Indian man, started screaming. "No blood in de store! No blood in de store! Get out! Get out!" I looked at my friend, as I was totally out of my league on this one. It was the first time I'd been out in New York City with a group of people (I can't call them friends, now can I?). The first time I'd ever been shot in the face. And the first time (but not the last) that I'd ever been screamed at by a small, irate Indian deli man.

"She got shot, for Pete's sake, don't you have some ice or something?" So the hospitable proprietor grabbed some napkins and a cup of ice, put his hand on my shoulder, and quickly steered us out of the store, down the steps, and in front of a liquor store, a much more appropriate backdrop for a shooting.

My friend patched me up a bit and, with my approval, put me in a cab and hurried off to her friends. I went straight back to my NYU medical student housing, took the elevator, let myself into a very dank, dark, mice-infested apartment, and sat on the bed.

We deduced that I had been shot with a pump or a BB gun as we called them growing up. This conclusion was arrived at because my face had not been blown to smithereens like it might have had it been a real gun. Likewise, it was a deeper injury than, say, a slingshot could commit. No wonder it didn't go through my cheek (and straight into my brain and blind me for life!). It made a perfectly round hole the size of a pencil eraser. In fact, if you didn't know better, you might have thought someone had simply ground a pencil eraser into my right cheek, albeit with crushing force. The next morning I had a giant, hard black bruise the size of a nickel with that eraser-sized hole smack dab in the middle. My right eye, while not black, had dark circles under it. I looked like a freak.

As I sat there in the room that night, I wrapped myself in my dad's college blanket. I stared straight ahead into the full-length mirror mounted on the wall. I held my hand to my cheek. My whole head was throbbing and I was all alone. I didn't cry. Not that I am opposed to crying–I cry a lot, for the record. I just sat there and thought to myself, "Wow, this is not what I expected living in New York would be like." It was an "aha" moment of epic proportions.

Later the next day, I went to the drugstore and stocked up on concealer. Concealer in a stick. Concealer in a bottle. Concealer in a tube. You name it, I bought it. I went home that night and practiced concealing my wound. It looked like a giant, oozing zit with a knot underneath. Which was better than it looking like a gunshot wound, I guess.

I didn't call my parents. If I had, they would have demanded I return home–that's how they would have rescued me and I definitely did not want to be rescued. And besides a short-lived, scabby, bruised cheek and later a small vague scar, it simply wasn't that big of a deal *at the time.* When Mom and Dad saw me later that summer, I concocted some tale about smog and pollution plugging my delicate pores. I turned my real-life, big-city horror story into a teenaged skirmish with a pimple.

But that "aha moment" stayed with me. It didn't change my desire to be in New York City or all I felt for the city. I had a resume to build, a city to explore, and an itch to scratch when it came to being on my own. But it was a pivotal instant for me, like at eighth-grade basketball tryouts when I realized not everyone would make the team, and I would probably be part of the "not everyone." Over the next two decades, there would be more "aha moments":

> Sometimes undeserving people will get promoted before you get promoted, and there is nothing you can do except silently seethe and be really snotty to them during staff meetings.
>
> Everyone can't be invited to everything and sometimes you won't be included. As someone with high social needs, that one really hurt. I don't always want to go, but I always want to be invited.
>
> Guys who tell you that they could never be married to someone so complex and interesting don't really love you . . . not at all. And you're probably not that complex and interesting, but rather high maintenance and whiny.
>
> Barfing on the shoes of someone you like is hard to overlook, and no matter how hard you will him to call you, he won't. Because you did puke on his brown suede bucks, after all.
>
> Try as you might, you can't be friends with a woman who swears that her farm animals speak to her. I mean, come on.

But I would have to say that the most compelling "aha moments" are when it comes to marriage. Ask any married couple, old or new, about an "aha moment" and they can reel them off quicker than they can recall their anniversary date. By "aha moment," I mean your own personal gunshot moment where perhaps you hold your face–or some other wound–and say to yourself, "Wow, this isn't what I thought it was going to be." And that moment is a crossroads of sorts. You realize that it's either going to be better than you thought, worse than you imagined, or most likely, just different than you ever dreamed. Like New York.

It can be startling. Like when my sister-in-law, who grew up in Saudi Arabia, realized my brother's incredible and deep repertoire of wit and observation was simply a constant riff on pop culture. He was ripping off music, books, television, and more, and she grew up in such a cultural vacuum that she thought it was all zany new content and that he was a riot. "I thought he was an original!" she said. "Are things different now that you know?" I asked. "In a way, but he's quick and he's funny and he still makes me laugh. And I love him. So I guess it doesn't matter."

My girlfriend Julia realized that the whole package of managing her cute guy included her husband's siblings, and that she would have to spend time with his family a lot of the time instead of her own. In fact, she had to miss a wonderful wedding party for her brother and his new wife because she had to entertain her hubby's family for Easter. "The resentment I felt at having to miss my family gathering to host my sister-in-law was enormous. And this had less to do with dealing with his family than with realizing that, although I prefer to always get my way, that just wasn't going to happen all the time anymore." So true, friends, so true.

There are some things that just don't matter, like a tiny little scar that doesn't really show anymore, because you're still in it for the long haul even when you realize that the person you love doesn't love the things you love–like sex, or your extended family. But what happens if your aha is of such a magnitude that you can't look away?

Like Brad, whose aha moment didn't involve me, but his first fiancée. Brad moved to DC after getting his political science degree. In a weird twist of fate he actually got a job in his major–which is less common than you might think. In fact, his biology major sister became a basketball coach. Like the thousands of true believers who go to Washington to change the world, Brad reveled in his Republicanism. He helped elect a Republican president, traveled overseas with the U.S. State Department, and of course, searched like the rest of us for that special someone.

He was smitten by this girl–a friend of a friend–who was sweet and smart and pretty. They began dating, and as things do, they got serious in a hurry. Soon they were living together then, shortly thereafter, engaged. And like so many of us, he got caught up in the idea of something. He was young, living in the nation's capital, working with and for powerful people. There were receptions on the Hill, happy hours at the Fox and Hound or the Hawk and Dove, and late nights at the Spy Club. He was having the time of his life. Except that he never stopped to think about what he was doing with his life.

Brad and his fiancée were very different. He was a Midwestern conservative and she was a West Coast liberal. He was raised an Episcopalian; she wanted to raise their children Jewish. His brother was an electrical engineer; her brother was a rock star–literally. As the plans for the wedding were laid out and the details coming together, Brad began having doubts about their long-term compatibility, and his decision to marry her. Nagging doubts gave way to full-fledged panic. Just cold feet, everyone has cold feet, he reassured himself. "This feeling is normal," he pleaded with himself. "It happens to everyone–right?"

One day he asked a mentor he frequently lunched with–how did you know your husband was *the one*? "I just did," she said. Aha. And that's when he knew that his fiancée wasn't. But how does one undo the kind of thing he'd done? How does one who can't return cold soup to the kitchen, or demand a nonsmoking hotel room, tell a wonderful woman and her great family that he can't go through with it? How do you let people who are sending you wedding gifts and making flight arrangements know that the gifts will have to be returned and travel plans canceled? How do you crush someone you truly care for? Well, you do it because you realize that it won't be better a year from now, or when you have kids, or after you've been married ten years.

People are always intrigued that Brad was engaged before, and they want to know the salacious details–don't all aborted weddings make a good story? Brad has always firmly declined to elaborate. "Why don't you want to talk about it?" I've asked him, as I was as guilty a rubbernecker as the next person. "Why?" he'd replied. "Why would you want to hear a story about how much I hurt someone? Why would you find fun or interest in that? I certainly didn't." Aha. Why indeed.

So there are some aha moments that demand action and there are some that demand silent respect. My aha moment when it comes to marriage? Oh, where to begin, friends, where to begin? Don't we all have a list of aha's lodged, just for kicks, somewhere in our memories next to the lovely photos of our wedding day?

But the most important aha moment from this marital experiment is this: Sometimes you gotta do it when you just don't want to. Just like you have to spend holidays with your in-laws, or a Sunday afternoon cheering on a team you could care less about. And that you need to do it with a happy heart . . . or as happy a heart as you can conjure up at the moment.

Because you know when you go to the dentist and you're sitting in the chair and you have that silly little bib pinned on you and the chronically cheerful hygienist with freaky long eyelashes (I know this because what other health practitioner gets that close to your face) asks you weird questions like if your health history has changed at all over the past year–as if that UTI last month can really impact your plaque buildup? And you're all tensed up before the hygienist even gets near your teeth with that weirdly long electronic plaque scraper that sounds like it will rupture your eardrums?

Well, that's the feeling I get these days when I have sex every day with Brad.

Right now, I so loathe the idea of having sex that I'm tense before I even change into my pajamas. It's by no means his fault, but we're nearing the end of this agreement, and all I really want to do is just crawl under the covers for once and go to sleep. But I can't, so I try, I really do. I think happy thoughts and sing happy songs in my head, but the fact remains: *I am tired of doing it!*

It seems that in the final stretch of sex there is this inverse correlation. The more unbearable it becomes for me, the more wonderful it becomes for Brad. Seriously, minus his pass earlier this month, on some days he couldn't be randier. I, on the other hand, am dragging myself to bed, sighing heavily, and falling dramatically into the pillows. "Let's get on with it," I mutter. And here he comes, bounding onto the bed, teeth freshly brushed and wearing a big grin–like your favorite golden retriever. How could we, nearing the end of our sex-every-day arrangement, have such incredibly different feelings about this?

"Could you stop grimacing?" Brad asked me one night.

"I'm not grimacing," I said between clenched teeth.

"Yes, you are. Could you pretend you're enjoying it?"

"How 'bout you just close your eyes," I suggested. He sighed huffily and did just that.

So this idea of us bonding, growing closer together, and connecting in new and more meaningful ways? Well, on that special evening in May all I could say to that was: "Whatever."

Because even on a bad day (and all told, there really haven't been that many), I can't even get credit. I can't go into a store and dramatically throw my hand to my brow and exclaim, "Wait on me this instant, can't you see I'm on the verge of collapse? I've been having *sex* with my husband *every day for nearly a year*!"

I can't go into work and say to a persnickety client, "Well,

I'm sorry you're not happy with this program, but I had the worst evening ever, because I had to have sex for the two hundred and fifty-eighth time this year! So stop your yammering, and fetch me a can of Diet Coke!"

You can't contribute this major nugget of information to your cocktail party conversations: "Yes, well, while you all were skiing in Vail this winter break, I was having sex every day with Brad. But enough of that, how was the base this year?"

You can't confide in your mother, "I'm sorry your ninety-year-old mother is so unbearably cranky. But if you really want to know what's unbearable, try having sex with your husband for ten straight months."

People cannot know my angst, not that they would feel much sympathy for me. It was my stupid idea, after all, to have this unending sex with my husband. Nope, daily sex with your spouse is a hidden cross to bear. Which is a new thing for me, really. All the burdens I usually bear are pretty obvious and hard to hide. Like managing my weight. Or rather mismanaging my weight. Or drinking too much at a cocktail party–now that's hard to camouflage. Even when I beg Brad to help me. "I told you to take me home instantly if I was overserved at the Barneses' cocktail party. What happened?"

"Sweetie, you were having such a good time doing your impersonation of your mother that I hated to spoil the fun."

"Well, next time, please feel free to spoil my fun and save some perfectly nice people from the need to avoid me the next time they see me at the dry cleaners."

So it was hard to complain about having sex with Brad. And

in reality I shouldn't complain at all. Yes, I made my bed, and now I must get laid in it.

So whenever I'm down in the dumps or stressed out–like I was nearly this entire month of May–I embark on one of my favorite stress relievers. I buy lipstick. Chanel lipstick. It always, always makes me feel better. I head to the mall and go straight to the Chanel counter, assessing all the well-coifed Chanel women in their chic black Chanel smocks. I don't need them, though, I have my Chanel therapy down to a science. I step up to the counter and look at all those gorgeous perfectly arranged tubes on the cosmetics counter and I immediately feel calm and centered. I am in wonder over the brilliant geniuses who created these colors and carefully numbered and named them. I admire the sleek, high-gloss black tube with the gold band that is the exact width of Brad's wedding ring. I roll the tubes around in my hand and I conjure up images of my life, Chanel-style–sleek, sophisticated, and mysterious (in other words, the polar opposite of my slobby, very average sex-every-day real life). I channel Coco herself as I try on shade after shade of reds, pinks, and corals, cocking my head from side to side in the mirror to see the brilliant colors from all angles. And I try to convince myself that while Coco and I look nothing alike, we do have similar coloring, and that her signature red would look just as timeless and chic on me (or maybe not). Coco said, "A girl must be two things–classy and fabulous," and after I leave the Chanel counter, I feel both for a bit. No. 17: Allure. No. 18: Vamp. Red No. 5. No. 81: Marilyn. No. 79: Rose Paradise. To name a few of my favorites. Ah, they sound so lovely, don't they?

Coco is to me a hero of sorts–incredibly fashion forward in her stubborn refusal to bow to fashion trends (à la how the Little Black Dress was born). She lied about her age, by ten years, if you can believe it. She dabbled in art, fashion, and cosmetics and generally did whatever she wanted, which was quite scandalous at the time. And she had those fabulous gi-normous sunglasses that I just love.

It's hard to feel classy and fabulous when you're forty and fatigued, but I did like to fantasize about what my life could be like if all I needed was an LBD, a tube of No. 18: Vamp, and some cab fare outta this life. Instead, I sighed, put on my sunglasses, pursed my Chanel lipstick–drenched mouth, tried to remember where I'd parked my big honkin' SUV, and drove home to have sex with my husband.

JUNE

Wedding Season

It was June twenty-fourth, and the last night of a family vacation at the beach. Only ten more days and our sex-every-day agreement would officially conclude. I was in bed, reading. Brad came to our room. I sighed, put down my book, and got ready, which really meant I just continued lying there.

Then I realized I had a wedgie, so I worked through that.

"Wow, that was really romantic, sweetie. I'm really attracted to you right now."

I looked at him with utter disbelief. "I'm sorry?"

"Geez, do you think you could try a little bit more?" he said.

"What do you mean?" I asked.

He sighed. "Could you pretend you're interested in this? I mean, could you woo me a bit?"

* * *

Try? Woo? What does he think I've been doing the last eleven months of my life? Intimacy every day is trying: It requires stamina, patience, personal grooming, and a work ethic I did not know I possessed. At least he never discovered that three-inch hair behind my knee that my razor has missed—the romance would be dead for sure. But 354 days of offering intimacy and all of a sudden he wants romance? I burst out laughing. I was giggling so hard that I had to turn away. But he was serious. I knew this because he said, "Honey, I'm serious."

I laughed harder. I mean, the irony of it all. I curled up into a ball, held my stomach, and screamed with laughter. After a minute, Brad cracked a smile.

"Are you telling me that after eleven months and twenty days of offering you no-strings-attached sex every day that you want something more?"

"I don't want more, I want better." Well, wasn't that dramatic.

"Excuse me, but could you clarify? What is better than having sex every day with your wife for an entire year?"

"Well, does it really count if you're just lying there, not that into it?"

Wait a darn minute, buster. We reviewed all this at the beginning of the agreement, and there was no discussion that "just lying there" was not in the spirit of The Gift. Besides, before this arrangement, there were plenty of times I was just "lying there" and I would venture to say that most married women across America have been just "lying there" for many, many years, perhaps decades. I would venture further to say that the term "just lying around" has its roots in the marital bed. In fact, I'm surprised it's not a piece of common marital advice. "When all else fails, just lie there."

Nevertheless, I tried harder. While wooing was out of the question, I did try to have an eventful little roll in which I was an active participant. It wasn't anything great, but it certainly wasn't the worst. Good enough would have to be good enough on this 354th day with my husband.

If marital advice was in scant supply when our mothers were starting out, it's certainly everywhere now. Talk shows, bookstores, girlfriends–everybody has an opinion on how to make a marriage work. But people are still getting divorced–is the advice lost on some of us, or is it just not enough?

Getting married is big business. Today, 2.4 million couples get married every year in the United States and it has become a $72 billion industry, according to www.theknot.com. Of course, June is the most popular month for getting married, and sure enough, this year rightly shouldn't have passed without receiving yet another gilded invitation. I have been to my share of weddings, starting way back in college. In fact, I have been a bridesmaid in ten weddings, not counting my friend Marcie's second and third trips to the altar. For a while there, I was indeed the perpetual bridesmaid.

Brad and I got engaged in the mountains. The elevated backdrop made up for the proposal–which was borderline pitiful. For some reason, all of Brad's experience in high school drama failed him and he simply froze. We were at a quaint bed-and-breakfast and we both knew it was coming (please, don't most women know when the proposal is coming?), but he literally couldn't get out the words. I guess it's sweet and a bit romantic when the love of your life says, "Uh, so you wanna get married?" while blushing a bright crimson color. No words about how this last year has been the most wonderful one of his life. No sentiments about our incredible future together. No mention of his dreams to have a family with me. No love notions about how incredibly fantastic and special I am. Just "Uh, so you wanna get married?" Well, the man has always been a straight shooter and indeed I did want to get married. We drank an entire bottle of champagne and I called my mother, who squealed with delight and set the entire wedding machine in motion that very second.

This year, another wedding announcement and invitation made their way through the family. While I vaguely thought that the whole of my generation had gotten married, in came the announcement that my first cousin was going to get hitched.

I adore my first cousin–she's young, smart, and vibrant and will make her very nice groom a terrific wife. My mom and I went to her wedding with my kids, and made a short weekend out of it. My brother and dad had long-standing plans and couldn't attend the wedding, so I gave Brad a pass on having to go, which he grabbed like a starving cat. It's funny–women love weddings and men just don't. In fact, my dad has been known to conveniently skip the actual wedding and strategically show up at the reception. When people comment on the ceremony, he nods along knowingly. "I know! Wasn't the music wonderful?" he chimes in as he heads to the buffet table. For men, weddings are boring unless it's a family member or best friend and even then the wedding is still boring, but there is an open bar to offset the serious stuff.

My cousin walked down the aisle, and I cried. I cry even if I'm sitting on the groom's side in the way back and I don't know the bride from Eve. I cry at how beautiful she looks. Even if she doesn't look *that* beautiful (and let's face it, some don't), she probably looks as good as she'll ever look. And I assume that she'll never look that wonderful again, so I cry a little tear of regret on her behalf. I cry as the music swells and the soloist crescendos and I think that this will be the last time this woman will ever, ever be the center of attention, and that the rest of her life will be spent negotiating happiness with another person. And I cry another little tear of regret on her behalf. (I hope someone did for me.) Then I cry at the sight of her dad walking her down the aisle and the overwhelming mix of emotions he must have. And I hope that the groom exceeds all that her dad wishes for her and I cry another tear, of regret, because I know somewhere along the way someone is going to be disappointed. And I cry, because as beautiful as she looks and as happy as she appears, she has no idea what's ahead. If she did, she might be crying along with me.

Instead, my cousin looked marvelously happy. After the ceremony, we walked from the church to the reception at a nearby museum. At that point, my cousin tucked a hot pink Gerbera daisy into her pretty chignon, and danced the night away in her bare feet. As my mother wrangled my children out onto the dance floor, I mused about just how long these sweet newlyweds would enjoy each other. I hoped it would be for a long, long time.

We all bring our "stuff" to marriage, and growing up in the seventies and eighties was not without its challenges. The feminist movement was gaining momentum and many of my childhood notions of marriage and relationships were changing at breakneck speed. Barbie and Cinderella were still around, but Barbie was a doctor now, and Cinderella could march on Washington. Women were pursuing careers dressed in ugly imitations of men's business attire–dark, masculine suits and floppy bow scarves.

I was encouraged to be a successful businessperson, and achieve high marks in every part of my life academically (which I did, on occasion). And while it was expected that I would marry–and marry well, whatever the heck that meant–I was not offered such stewardship in that area.

My father issued me one rule: If I got married before I turned twenty-seven, he would not pay for the wedding. It was a gift, really. First of all, I felt off the hook in a way. I graduated from college, moved to New York, and never gave a thought to having a boyfriend or finding one. I did not have a boyfriend or find one in college or in New York, but I did have a ball and never felt any pressure to seriously date, much less settle down. A regular date now and then would have been nice, but overall I was able to experience a bit of independence and a life on my own. That was a good thing. And while my parents were secretly terrified that I would meet someone in New York and stay there forever, perhaps they knew that I needed a bit of seasoning before I could make a mature decision about whom to marry.

So for me, getting married early was not in the cards, through fate or choice, and Brad and I married when I was thirty-one. I do know four people who married early, to their high school sweethearts–my mother, my mother-in-law, my cousin Jenn, and my college roommate Diane. For everyone else, I shudder to think about the trajectory of their lives, including mine, if they married their first love so young. I was a late bloomer, and late bloomers should never marry a high school sweetheart because they still have some finishing up to do. If you want a depressing twist on *It's a Wonderful Life* (which is already depressing, if you ask me), imagine your life if you had married your high school sweetheart. If I had married Alex, and I really thought I would, who knows how crazy and miserable I might be and he certainly would be. So I am always intrigued when people marry their high school or college sweethearts and it works out because you're making really, really important decisions and you're still really, really young. How do they do that?

So as I matured (ever so slowly, like those plants that only bloom every seven years or so), I started working on the list of qualities I must have in a mate. Women do this whether or not we admit it, and hopefully the list grows and matures as we do. For example, my list from my twenties included stupid mandatories like must be "a scratch golfer" and "from the South." I thought these two traits were extremely important. Go figure. People might scoff at the list but, remember, often your mate is only as good as the requirements you put on it.

I remember a dear friend of mine calling me in tears one day. This was during Marriage No. 1, and her first husband was on her case about her weight. "He says he's not attracted to me now that I've gained a little weight," she sobbed into the phone. This is a good time to mention that this friend of mine is a knockout and she and Hubby No. 1 met at the gym where they both worked. Hubby No. 1 was a nice enough guy, I guess. But I think the most important thing he had going for him was that he was smoking hot. "I can't believe he married me for my looks!" she wailed into the phone. "Sweetie, tell me this–why did you marry him?" I wanted to add, "It wasn't because he was a brain surgeon, now was it?" But I didn't. She had married Hubby No. 1 for many of the same reasons he had married her, I suppose. And yes, she loved him and all that stuff, too. But she had made a list, and then she outgrew her list, and once she realized it, it was too late.

Even though I had purged my list of some of the shallower requisites and updated it with more substantial ones, Brad still didn't fit the mold. Sure, he wasn't from the South and wasn't a scratch golfer, but he also came from divorced parents, went to a college I had never heard of, wasn't bust-a-gut funny, wasn't short and stocky, and so on. Why did Brad measure up? He fit a mold I hadn't tried before–decent, smart, loving, kind, interesting, and incredibly devoted to me. Yes, that last one was a new one.

We choose men for lots of the same reasons they choose us—attractiveness and attraction, employment, family background, faith, religion. But intimacy compatibility? Well, that's generally present in spades at the beginning and it never occurred to me that could change. It is difficult to imagine ourselves twenty years from now, married with kids, a job, a house, and a very mediocre sex life. In fact, it is difficult to imagine all the bumps in the road ahead of a married couple that could affect our sex lives: illness, unemployment, stress, infertility, fertility, financial woes, infidelity, success, aging. Let's face it: We never know what life is going to throw at us, and all and more of these issues can knock a relationship sideways, and spin intimacy completely out of the consideration set.

Most of us don't know any of this, we get married anyway, and we enter the covenant of marriage with unlikely expectations. Whether your parents were married or divorced, it seems many of us are woefully unprepared for all that is demanded, expected, and negotiated in marriage. It is an unwieldy lifelong assignment, and it brings out the absolute best and worst in us all. Premarital counseling seems like a noble endeavor, and many churches and synagogues and other places of worship require that you attend some sort of workshop in order to get married there. But there have been times when I thought that psychic counseling may have provided greater value.

Brad and I had premarital counseling that consisted of, among many things, taking the Myers-Briggs Type Indicator, which I really advise against, especially if the invitations have already gone out. I mean, when you find out that you and your future spouse could not be more incompatible, isn't it a tad too late already? That wasn't entirely the case for us, but I did find out that I am an extrovert and Brad is an introvert. The important insight we got out of those tests is that we "recharge differently." Apparently, being around him (and other people) recharges me, while Brad needs to recharge . . . without me.

Were we discouraged from getting married? Of course not. We had momentum on our side–the whole wedding thing had taken on a life of its own. That wedding was *happening*, just ask my mother. And we were so darn in love that we wouldn't let any differences get in the way of us getting married–we could work through them, gosh darn it. Rather, they should really have done a sexual compatibility test. Brad will want sex and will resent having to ask for it. I will not want to have sex after two babies and fifty-hour workweeks and will resent having to have it. Now, talk among yourselves . . .

So instead, I would like to suggest Marriage Internships. Unlike living together before you get married (which I still think is a shaky idea despite my feminist views about many things, because it lacks permanence), you and your fiancé live with another couple. Preferably in a small house, modestly furnished with young kids. It's kind of like auditing a class. You spend day in and day out observing this couple navigate jobs, house, babies, cleaning, social lives, and each other. Sometimes it's bad. Sometimes it's good. Sometimes it's just life. It's a hard, close-up dose of reality. If after that you're still smitten with your partner and the idea of marriage, then give it go.

I asked my mom once what was her secret to her long and

happy marriage. She glibly replied that she had picked the right guy. Well, how did you know? I probed. "I don't know, sweetie, I loved him. Plenty of my friends thought they had a good one, too, but it was the wrong one." Luck of the draw, God's hand, call it what you want, but she was grateful for it. Brad's parents were also high school sweethearts and they divorced when he was ten, so who's to say?

Back then, people tended to stick close to home and marry young. That way, you didn't know much about the great big world you were missing when you married *Most Likely to Succeed*, who became *Drinks Too Much and Can't Hold Down a Job.* In some ways, is life better if you don't know how many choices eluded you?

Nowadays, you go away to camp, you travel every summer, you go to college, you travel abroad, you have different internships in different cities, you have several different jobs, again in several different cities. You have global friends, global experiences, and a global love life. You are exposed to so much, how in the world can you narrow your options and choose the one person with whom you'll spend the rest of you life? It's simply too much. Choices can kill the ability to make basic and rational choices that won't later haunt you till your dying days.

My friend Cindy thinks there are too many choices available to us all and research says she's right. Apparently, Wal-Mart can be bad for us as we spend exponentially more hours making low-impact decisions because there are too many choices. Frivolous choices that don't necessarily enhance or change our lives. Sunscreen. Baby wipes. Shampoo. And the potato chip aisle? Forget it. Anyone remember the Charlie Chip Man? He rode around in a Charles Chip postal truck painted yellow and brown and delivered a tin of chips to your house–plain, BBQ, and sour cream and onion. Surely one would fit the bill, and if it didn't, we were better off anyway.

For some of us, life narrows our options. And maybe that's not so bad. All the options could give us ulcers. But my dad is a big believer in options. He's made a career out of developing, honing, and creating options for himself and for our family. Networking, building, and planning what will come next. The man could teach a master class on *options*.

When applying to college, you want to have options, he told me. Don't put all your eggs in one basket, and you will always have options. When you're looking for a job, leave yourself some options. When you're in a job, stay focused and work hard. But remember, you always have options. Options are a reward of sorts. Hard work, smart decisions, and commitment yield choices. And having choices means you're not stuck. Stuck in a job, stuck in a place, or stuck in a rut. Choices are a good thing. But how about stuck in marriage? Getting married is antithetical to options. Marriage means you've made a choice and you've decided there are no better options. But despite the fact that marriage and options don't really jibe, my dad was still a fan of the institution.

Now here my father and I are, standing in the foyer of First Baptist Church at approximately 5:57 P.M. on Saturday, June 20, 1998. I am, as you might guess, dressed in white. My dad is quite handsome and looks smashing in his tux. The bridesmaids have already made the march. The trumpeter is in the balcony above our head preparing for my dramatic entrance and my mother is at the front of the church in one of the three mother-of-the-bride gowns purchased for a day she thought might never come. And I am sweating right through a very, very expensive wedding dress. The wedding planner is fluffing my train and Dad turns to me.

"You don't have to do this, you know, honey. Just say the word and we're out of here," he says.

Say what?

Who is this guy? He looks like my dad and sounds like my dad, but no dad of mine in his right mind would offer his thirty-one-year-old daughter the chance to skip out on the wedding of her dreams and the party of a lifetime—*mere seconds before the walk down the aisle.* Not in front of all these people and not on his tab. He must be whacked . . . or drunk.

So again—*say whaaat?*

"I just want you to know that, no matter what, you always have options."

My eyes are as big as the gorgeous pink roses stuffed into my very heavy bouquet and I'm wondering if my makeup is melting off my face. Now, I suppose it is better to discuss marital options before one has actually said "I dos," but my goodness, this was cutting it close. I am about to march down the aisle, publicly declare my undying love to Brad, and promise to cherish him 'til death do us part. Whether or not we should have added lamb to the carving station, well, those are options I can discuss.

My maid of honor is nearly making the turn. The wedding planner is pulling at my arm, positioning Dad (who is quite sober and sane) and me in front of the giant double doors that are about to swing open and reveal my sweaty, melting self to all the world–or to at least five hundred people standing in the church. You know those moments people have when they think they're going to die–the ones where their life flashes before their eyes (and they sometimes faint)? Well, that happens to me, without the fainting part. I have flashbacks to my childhood (happy), visions of swimming slowly underwater with my hair all crazy and undulating around my head (peaceful), visions of eating birthday cake (tasty), vision of holding hands with Brad (joyful), and visions of dating (horrific). Well, those visions of dating are what snap me out of it. I shake my head, take a deep breath, get myself centered, and contemplate what the heck has just happened.

And then it comes to me. I realize that, true to form, my father has simply given me a gift. He's telling me that no amount of money spent or people assembled is more important than my happiness. And up until that very minute, that very second, in fact, there has been nothing that we couldn't undo. He's offering me a mulligan if I need it. And at that very moment, I'm overcome with emotion for my dad–the very first man I ever loved. But I don't need a do-over on this one. In fact, I feel really good about this option. So the trumpeter starts his gig, the wedding planner gives us the signal, the doors crank open, and I turn to my dad and break out the best smile I've got. "Thanks for the offer, Dad. Let's go."

Perhaps it is the power of choice, and possibilities for newer and better, that can chip away at the previous choices you've already made. For instance, how long do you love your first couch, your first car, your first job, your first husband?

Newer and greater things come out all the time, and in our consumer society, it's practically sanctioned that we swap out the old with the new. So it might feel as though you're still hanging on to a choice that you made from 1992 when you were so young and stupid, and maybe life without your husband or wife would be so much, well, so much brighter and shinier and *newer*?

And perhaps that's the scariest thing–despite the commitment we made for better or for worse, there is still the idea that our spouse could wake up one day and decide on an upgrade. We know it happens, but we don't think it's going to happen to us, especially when we're young and vibrant and "new." But when we hit forty, well, we're not that shiny and new anymore, are we, despite forty being the new thirty? And the marriages we were sure would go kaput are still going strong. And the marriages that sometimes seemed impenetrable suddenly implode.

Working in PR has its moments. On occasion you get to do some neat things like meet your favorite B-list actors–Kim Alexis, anyone? Go on great trips–North Dakota, for example. Or you get to coordinate over-the-top firework shows or even blow up buildings. Recently, I helped blow up an old coliseum in our city. It was actually an implosion; the coliseum would collapse inwardly with force, as a result of the external pressure being greater than the internal pressure. In this case, complete obliteration of something that once stood for something. Are we all party to some sort of implosion in our marriages? Do we sometimes collapse inwardly as external pressures bear down on us? Do we contribute in some way to the destruction of something that was, at one time, useful?

Believe it, it's incredibly stressful blowing up a building, and we worked all hours to prepare to implode a giant structure so that my client could build something shiny, new, and useful. We had worked months and months on the strategy to implode this building. Where would the crowds stand? Which VIPs would push the button? What would we say about the old and the new? It ran on ESPN, Fox News, and more than seven hundred stations around the country. It was voyeurism at its finest hour–short, sweet, and utterly complete.

We imploded the old space because it wasn't needed; but we really imploded the building because we had outgrown it. Do we do that in relationships? Do we implode them, too, when we've outgrown them and it's time to move on to something else? Of course we do, especially when we're young and we lack maturity and insight to value things that have the worn patina of time.

According to the press packet, there were 524 charges timed to explode in 52 delays of 500 milliseconds, split into two sequences running concurrently to reduce the concussion from the blast. Overall, the process was expected to take about 13 seconds to complete, dropping the roof onto the floor and toppling some of the walls. In one tiny moment a building that took years to build was reduced to rubble. When relationships end, people can sometimes pin it to one tiny charge. Others say the 524 charges exploded in such subtle milliseconds that they didn't know it had imploded until they were standing in the rubble rubbing their head from the concussion of it all.

When a relationship collapses, the voyeur in us sneaks out. We want to know, we have to know: What went wrong? What did you do? How did it happen? Why did it happen? For some, it's shameful nosiness. For others, it's a need to know so that we can protect ourselves against such heartache and tragedy–and it still comes across as shameful nosiness, doesn't it?

But even if we do know what happened and why it happened, what do we do then? If knowledge is power, how do we use it to our marital benefit, and do we even know how? You don't have to be a marital pioneer to know that infidelity can cripple a marriage, for example. But what about the little triggers or charges we could avoid every day that might save our relationship a little bit–do we have the sense and the discipline to steer clear of those? I often think about my wedding day, waiting with my dad for those heavy church doors to swing open and for my life as a married person to officially commence. I could have jumped in the car that day and created an implosion of another kind. So here I am.

Independence Day!

"Did you have a happy birthday, honey?" I sang out as I woke up on July Fourth.

I rolled over, gave him a smooch, and grabbed my robe. "Where are you going?" he mumbled from under a pillow.

"I'm getting up. It's a beautiful new day! Sleep in if you want."

"I think I will. And I know it's a new day, thank you. Could you please not be so happy about it?" He rolled away from me.

Happy is an understatement. I mean, come on, I had done it!

I offered to be intimate with my husband every day for a year and *I did it!* My first day off was Independence Day, July Fourth–how incredibly appropriate. Let freedom ring, friends! This marked both the birth of this journey, and the independence from it. I was relieved, I was giddy, I was downright ebullient with the notion that I didn't have to have sex today!

When we had kicked off this arrangement, I wasn't sure where we would end up after this daily affair. While I woke up in the same place as I had exactly twelve months ago, to the day–in my bedroom in my parents' house on a mountain vacation–I was not emotionally in the same place. I had gone from feeling like the best, most tuned-in wife in America, to the thoughtful Professor Oz. "Well, what have you learned, Dorothy?"

My perky little bounce had less to do with the fact that I was free from daily sex (okay, maybe a little). I was bursting with a deep satisfaction that I had carried through on this gift. "I did it, I did it, I did it," I sang under my breath as I moved around the bedroom that morning. Brad knew I was pleased with myself, but I didn't need to flaunt it. After all, reaching Day 366 of this arrangement didn't exactly make him Mr. Happy Pants. But there are some things–like kids growing up or hair getting gray–that happen regardless of my level of involvement. And then there are things that require me to show up and do the work–like learning how to play the flute, getting a high school diploma, getting married, and giving this gift. And I have to say I was pretty darn proud of all my hard work. Soooo, "I did it, I did it, I did it!"

We had made intimacy routine, rote, customary. Sure, we had managed to throw in a couple of lovely no-kids, weekend-away connections (our awesome trip to the winery) that added some flavor and fun, but for the most part we turned the occasional into the daily. And it was wonderful, this daily date with Brad–even after twelve months of habitual snuggling, smooching, and yes, sex. For sure there were days when I was sick of the sex–I was tired of the same old thing, I just wanted my own space, or I didn't really feel the mojo all the time. But I was amazed to discover that I was never once sick of Brad. In a way, it was as if I have been reintroduced to this nice man I had married. "Charla, I'd like you to meet the person whom you vowed to cherish and honor. His name is Brad." And likewise, "Brad, this is your wife, Charla. You might see her every day, but here she is . . . with you at this moment each day . . . with no distractions."

I am ashamed to admit a year ago there were days when I was quite distracted and could get quite bogged down in what Brad was or wasn't doing to step up as a husband and a father. I really had neither the time nor tolerance to contemplate Brad as a person. But this daily gift unfolded many layers of surprising generosity in me. Instead of worrying about what I wasn't getting from Brad this past year, it made me wonder–besides intimacy, what else was Brad *not* getting from me? Daily intimacy brought some humanity to our marriage that I didn't know was missing. You know how those oxygen masks are designed to drop out of the ceiling of an airplane if needed? I wish something like that could happen in a marriage. Because just as we can suffer from oxygen deprivation, marriages can suffer from intimacy deprivation. And like me, you might not even know it until you start to turn blue.

A few years ago I was at the mall getting the battery replaced in my watch. I was waiting patiently and they finally called my name. I headed to a secured window at the back of the store where they handed me my watch in a black velvet drawstring bag. I reached for my wallet and the salesperson put her hand on my wrist and said to me, "No charge today, just pay it forward." "I'm sorry?" I said. "You know, pay it forward." Ohhhhh. Yes, it was about the time of said movie and I had to admit I was immediately touched, completely sucked into this whole idea of paying forward kindness and goodwill. In fact, I couldn't believe someone had picked me! Had thought me worthy enough to pay it forward! Had seen something in me that made her believe I could keep the tradition going!

As I walked out of the store into the mall atrium, I was quite caught up in the moment. I was overcome by the desire to pay it forward . . . right that moment. So looking around the mall, I spied a woman standing in front of the fountain. I raced over. She was perched on the side holding a large bulky handbag under her arm. It was hard to tell her age . . . she was definitely older than me but younger than my mom. She looked to be waiting for someone. "Hello!" I announced loudly. She blinked hard and looked at me. "I'd like to buy you some ice cream!" I declared, louder than I probably wanted. The lady looked around and pulled her handbag a bit closer. She squinted as she looked at me as though she should know me. "Um, no thank you."

"No really," I responded. "I really want to buy you ice cream . . . why don't we walk over to the Food Court and I'll buy you any flavor you want."

The woman looked at me like I was some kind of mall stalker. Meanwhile, I was working hard to close the deal and it was all just coming apart at the seams. I started to blabber to her about how I was trying to pay it forward because the woman at Tiffany who fixed my watch was so generous and I couldn't break the "pay it forward" chain. I kept insisting over and over to just let me buy her some freakin' ice cream . . . or at least let me give her the money so she could buy her own ice cream . . .

She walked off and I trailed behind her for a few steps, calling out to her, still trying to buy her some damn ice cream. In the end, I was left standing there feeling like I had been stood up by humanity, when I was only trying to pay it forward.

I realized that despite my good intentions, I still appeared like some freak mall stalker (and only by grace did I pick a woman of age . . . can you imagine if I had approached some teenager or kid with my ill-planned scheme?). I had not taken the time to think through the proposition and what it might mean. In many cases, good intentions without proper thoughtfulness make for a giant embarrassing mess or a situation where you are either arrested . . . or escorted off mall property.

Embarking on this intimacy-every-day arrangement would not have worked either if I had not planned properly. While I knew I wanted to offer Brad intimacy every day, I had to slow down and think through the logistics, the ramifications, the planning and scheduling, the promise of what I was actually offering–and what it would require from me. Was I paying it forward? Perhaps. Although the concept of paying it forward involves helping strangers for the overall good of society, I was working closer to home by reaching out to my husband for the good of our marriage. But it doesn't make the concept less poignant or less meaningful, does it?

I am not naïve enough to think that the universal panacea to all marital woes is more sex. What I am suggesting is that frequent intimacy in a stable relationship with a spouse or partner you love and care about brings about a near all-over conversion of sorts, or at least it did for me. I was certainly invested in our marriage before we did this (as one would have to be to embark on such a crazy ride), but I have never been more invested in Brad as a husband and partner than I was during this year. Being intimate daily forced me to be. Before last year, I would have told you that a regular intimate relationship is a nice thing to have–it's icing on the cake of a great marriage. Not anymore. Regular intimacy in my marriage is now a requisite. I didn't appreciate what Brad really needed in this kind of intimacy and I had no idea what *I* was missing. Nearly every day for a year I invested in a physical connection that paid off in emotional spades–we communicated better, we talked more, we had more fun (between the sheets and out of them), and we were teammates that connected more. There is no denying that this might be the best year of our marriage . . . yet.

Life can be divided up into fragments: infancy, early childhood, school years, college age, working life, marriage, parenthood, retirement; but each of us has moments that stick out in our lives, and define a year, or a decade. The eighties, for me, were all about bad hair and cheesy music. The nineties were all about becoming an adult, and being out on my own. The early 2000s were about starting a family. But the year we both turned forty, hmmmm, how would I look back upon that?

The summer I was fourteen I arrived home from sleep-away camp. Coming home from camp can be such a letdown. In some ways you are happy to be home, sleep in your own bed, and be around your own stuff. On the other hand, summer camp is way more fun than hanging with your ten-year-old brother at the pool, waiting for all your other friends to come home from summer camp. My parents picked me up in the church parking lot, loaded my dirty laundry into the trunk, and I hopped inside.

"Hey. Anything happen while I was gone?" I asked. My parents turned down the eight-track, glanced at each other and then at me. "Well, we did get cable," my dad said.

"And your cousin Denise got shot," added my mom.

Wow. That was weird. I knew there was a right way to respond to this statement, but my mind was just not tracking properly–I was running on a total of fifty hours sleep over a two-week period, had an itchy rash from icky lake water, and had run out of my Body on Tap shampoo halfway through the session.

"Is she okay?"

"Um, yes," they responded.

"What happened?"

"Someone broke into the house and shot her."

I mean, this sounded like a bad case on *Andy Griffith.* I demanded that Andy and Barney get to the bottom of this and right now! It was so weirdly strange and obviously troubling.

I personally had never known anyone to get shot before (little did I know I was going to get shot in New York–how weird is that?). This was new territory.

That summer simply became known as "The Summer Denise Got Shot." It just as easily could have been "The Summer of MTV" as we did get cable that summer and that was fairly life-altering. It became an emotional benchmark–a year of initiations–summer camp, cable television, and people you love getting hurt.

Years later, the season Brad and I are in has become a benchmark of sorts, and I feel it deserves some kind of moniker. "The Year We Saved Our Marriage"? Nah, overblown–things were going fine, at least I thought so until things got so much better. "The Year We Had Sex Till We Thought We Would Croak"? Too over-the-top, and applicable only to me. "The Year Brad Walked Around with a Stupid Grin on his Face"? Maybe . . . "The Year Wifey Lost Her Marbles"? No, we need to save that one for later, maybe when I turn forty-five. "The Year Charla Cracked the Code on Her Marriage"? Hmmmm, we might be getting somewhere.

But despite my little "I rock!" self-congratulatory dance, I worry about what can *possibly* come for us as a couple after daily intimacy for a year? At the end of the day, we're still an average, now middle-aged couple who are still susceptible to the ups and downs that life throws at us. I mean, it's not like we can have sex every day *forever* . . . can we? (The answer is no, no, no, NO!) We have to figure out what we can do next.

Brad and I started out together as a rather smug couple.

When we were engaged, we had a great sense of self-satisfaction. We're "different," we told ourselves. We wouldn't be like those other couples who bickered all the time, we told ourselves, as we listened to another couple bickering. We wouldn't be like those other couples who sat in stony silence at restaurants, we told ourselves, as we watched a couple sit in stony silence. We wouldn't be the couple whose world revolved around children and 6:30 P.M. bedtimes . . . puhleeze, not us. And we certainly would not be a couple that, slowly and ever so slightly, drifted away from a life of intimacy because our sex life rocked! No, we considered ourselves an enlightened couple. We would be different. We had too much respect for ourselves and for each other to have just any old marriage. (Cue the laugh track.)

No one aspires to be that couple who bickers all the time, or who sits in stony silence in a restaurant, or who drops everything–even friends and family–to have a baby in bed by dusk. None of us aspires to a bad marriage or a thorny relationship with a spouse. No one intends to neglect a marriage. And no one intends to get married and have little or no intimacy. It often just happens, sometimes when we're not looking and sometimes right in front of our eyes. And that's when we realize that being married is really quite humbling. I went from smug to humble in about 365 days–the same amount of time as this little everyday gift. It was a swift reality check when you think about it. I went from realizing that I am not only *not* different from everyone else, but also that I am painfully, laughably, *comically* exactly like everyone else. I fell out of touch with my husband and had too many moments when the kids came first and too many nights when I fell in bed exhausted and depleted.

So, back to Oz. My girlfriends are dying to know: What did I learn? What will I do differently now that I "know"? While I'm not a therapist or a marital expert, I did take one for the gals' team over this past year. Sure, there were some incredible personal benefits, but what I learned was too important not to share, too life changing to keep to myself. I spent a year down in the trenches of intimacy, friends. It was hot, it was steamy, and many times, it was very redundant. Here is what I know:

I discovered that despite our busy lives, I *do* have time for quality intimacy on a regular basis. If I can assemble twenty-four goody bags for a birthday party, do four loads of laundry, answer a few e-mails, shower, empty the dishwasher, take a conference call, and make all the beds before I take my kids to preschool, I can figure out how to take twenty minutes to get up close and personal with Brad. I have time for quality intimacy because I need it as much as Brad needs it.

I discovered that sometimes, even if I'm tired, or not interested at that moment, or distracted by a dozen other things, I can't overanalyze whether I want to, whether we should, and what's in it for me. I just need to say *yes.* I just have to put on my big girl panties and be intimate with my husband. And I've realized that he will do the same for me. The daily tug-of-war in marriage didn't start in my lifetime; it was around when Eve was offering Adam a fruit bowl. Because it takes two. Because I married a person with feelings and a sex drive and a desire to connect. Because I signed on for this, so I can't be surprised or resentful Brad wants something, even when it's not at the top of my list. And I not only have to participate, I need to thoughtfully initiate and really mean it.

I discovered that despite my stellar performance this year, I can't rest on my laurels. I realize that while I had sex with my husband nearly every day for a *whole year,* a year from now it won't count. Remember the whole time value equation . . . My relationship, in some ways, is only as good as my last tryst. Which is okay, because it all makes Brad really, really, kidlike happy. If you want to see what an adult Disney World would be like (and I don't mean that in a raunchy kind of way), have sex with your husband more often. Brad was practically giddy–only a hat with mouse ears would have made the picture more complete.

I discovered that our house is no longer fraught with tension because we're no longer silently or verbally negotiating whether or not we'll have sex that day, that week, or that month. We're both more relaxed and comfortable, and for every married woman out there, that idea has to be a huge stress reliever. Brad likes to think there is less urgency on his end and I think there is less pressure on mine. We both know that intimacy is now part of the landscape of our relationship and we've both lightened up.

An aside: You might think this past tension would have led to some loud confrontations, but here is the funny thing. Before The Gift, Brad and I didn't fight much, and when we did, we didn't do it very well. I don't mean there wasn't conflict; it was just low simmering conflict, like a pot of hard-boiled eggs on the stove. This was due primarily to Brad's passive-aggressive nature and burning desire for peace, and my chronic frustration that after all these years he can't read my mind. (For example: How could he not know that I'm totally stressed out by this church commitment and I just need him to get the kids dressed and out the door–*now!?*) It's not that he acquiesced to me as much as he simply shut down, went on autopilot, and flew underneath my stormy fury. I would go into my seething silent treatment mode and after a few hours–or a few days–we were exhausted. After things had cooled, I would force him to talk to me about whatever my beef was, and we would haggle through some sort of weak resolution.

Sometimes we would try to "talk through things," but the bottom line is that I take criticism better than he does. I find this hysterically funny as there are not many areas where I trump Brad, and most are pretty lame, albeit useful. Let's see, I have better penmanship, I am a far better gift wrapper, I can cook (which is very, very important to us all), I can multitask with the best of them (but this is simply a gift of my gender) . . . and I take criticism far better. And it's not like I even take criticism all that well–just relative to him, I'm freakin' Mother Teresa.

Brad thinks that criticism is an indictment of his character, and it offends him to the core of his being (remember, bringing up errant nose hair was almost cause for couples arbitration). It truly wounds him. I have found that if I preface criticism with some assuring words of support, it helps. This goes something like this: I place my hands gently on his shoulder and I look him deeply in the eyes.

"I want to tell you something. But I don't want you to be

alarmed, I am not planning to file for divorce over this, and I don't love you less . . . but could you please consider not putting the grass clippings in a spare trash can to compost in our closed garage, as the compost breeds maggots and a really bad smell?" I then hug him and loudly affirm, "I love you."

Sometimes it works, sometimes not, and he snarkily reminds me that perhaps I should be thankful someone around here is doing some yard work for a change.

In light of this I discovered that our daily tryst forced me not to be mad at Brad. Believe me, I can't. I think Brad–and probably most men–could still be intimate even when there's some argument or disagreement brewing. I mean, aren't there some great movies based solely on the meager premise of "makeup" sex? I couldn't have hopped in the hay even once if I was peeved at some spousal transgression. Picture a moment of intimacy with someone who only moments before did/said something that rubbed you every which way the wrong way. See, it doesn't compute, does it?

Sex wasn't going to happen if I was totally cranked up about something. I didn't have it in me and we both knew it. So instead we were required to be pretty nice and pleasant to each other so that our moments of intimacy were real, genuine, and actually consummated. As Brad's yearlong gift progressed, I realized that I'd become a lover, not a fighter. Cheesy puns aside, it's worthy to note because I had to be on my best behavior all the time, not just behind closed doors. I must admit I wasn't counting on having to be nice most *all of the time.*

So as a follow-up to what I thought was an incredibly generous gesture of daily intimacy, I ended up giving even more—something I would not have thought remotely possible 365 days ago: I was crafted into a more gracious spouse (some days by the skin of my teeth, I might add). I became a kinder, gentler wife because of all the things that this experience forced me to do and think about during the course of my day. Not just the logistics, although they were important, but that we needed to work to stay in each other's favor so that we (well, really I) could deliver on this kind of connection. I was more thoughtful, more attentive, gentler in how I treated Brad because I knew that regular intimacy required me to be in a fairly good place emotionally.

In the old days, the stars might have been aligned in our favor: A great day with Brad would lead into a great evening with Brad would lead into a great intimate tryst with Brad. Accidental or not, one good thing led to another and we ended up with a nice intimate bond. But this past year, I had to align the stars myself. I couldn't wait on luck, a free moment, or let's face it, some nice wine. I learned that lifelong intimacy requires a kind of cushiony kindness and gentle awareness that allows us to come together and into a welcoming, safe, and intimate place.

Some people love to bake because baking is all about preciseness. There is little room for improvisation because baking is really a science. A cake rises because all the ingredients blend together to work in *exact* proportions. If you follow a baking recipe with meticulous care, measure out the ingredients with accuracy, and follow through with faithful diligence, you can bake the perfect soufflé. As my girlfriend, who is a great baker, once said, "Baking isn't that hard . . . you just have to pay attention and always, always, always follow the directions." And then there is cooking. Cooking is a bit looser, it allows for a bit more creativity, and it's open to translation. We probably all start a pot of chili with the same basic ingredients but then we rely on our wits and our personal palate to finish the pot to our preference. Well, you know where this is going . . .

Marriage is, of course, more like cooking. We are all working off the same recipe, but we improvise and invent and create something that tastes good to us. And while I love jalapeño peppers, you, not so much. So to match up two individuals in a committed relationship and blend wants and needs and expectations into something with just the right flavor, well, I can only say that we're each on our own.

But my girlfriends are looking for a number. Girls like to benchmark. We should exercise three to five times a week; we should eat two to three servings of fruit each day; a few glasses of red wine weekly; a cut and color every eight weeks; a mammogram and Pap annually. Numbers provide a yardstick against which we can measure ourselves, our health, our efforts . . . but our relationships? Is there a perfect recipe, so to speak: How much sex is enough sex to keep your marriage and your partner happy? So here's my recipe for making your own little intimacy stew. The magic number is . . . drumroll please . . .

Twice whatever you're doing now.

That's right. However often you're doing it, double it. And six months from now, double it again. Intimacy with our spouses should be at the top of our list all the time, and if we're doing something wack-a-doodle like doubling the amount of sex we're having, it means we're force ranking it and it will always be at the top of the list. (And for all you bakers who want the exact measurement . . . well, I'm sorry to tell you you're going to have to figure that out for yourselves.)

And if that just sounds too crazy, don't worry about it. I mean, what do I know? I'm just some kooky gal who aspired to have sex every day with her husband for a year . . . clearly, I'm deluded.

I recently saw in a movie that the reason we get married is because we need someone to bear witness to our lives. That we need someone who can testify to our living, our experiences, to the fact that we were, indeed, here at all. Regular intimacy with Brad is bearing witness up close and personal and is proof that we were not only here, but also alive . . . and very together.

"So happy birthday, honey. I really mean it," I offered up at the end of a day full of Independence Day festivities, and kissed him gently.

"Thanks, sweetie. It's been a great day and a great year and I love you," Brad said. "How about we go upstairs for a little L-O-V-E?"

Well, how about it!

Afterword

Dear Reader:

It always bugs me to hear a really great story (and I'm hoping that's what you thought this was) and still have questions. Some famous literary biggity wiggity out there might say that's exactly what makes a good piece of writing–it leaves you with unanswered questions, it prompts you to ponder and reflect, it keeps you up at night with niggly little points. *Ach*, who needs that, girls? We all need our sleep now, don't we? Besides, sometimes I simply need things all tied up in a nice little bow so that I might move on to the next thing. Closure, even a wee bit, is a good thing.

So this is where Brad and I are today:

First, I must report that we are not having sex every day. It was mostly fun for a year (remember May?), but alas, readers, not a long-term gig for me nor, it ends up, for Brad. I think Brad put it perfectly when he said, "Sex every day is not a sustainable model. But neither is sex hardly ever."

Which leads to my second point. I am happy to report that we are intimate a whole lot more than "hardly ever." And that is a very, very good thing for the both of us. It's warm, it's fun, and it's created an opportunity for comfortable dialogue regarding that elephant in the living room we called intimacy. Case in point: Brad and I were actually discussing our revised "intimacy schedule" after we ended our daily intimacy schedule in July.

"I think we should schedule it–how about every Monday, Wednesday, Friday?" I offered, the planner in me coming out strong with my hand poised and ready to pencil in a little "s" on every Monday, Wednesday, and Friday in my Kinko's calendar. We had decided that three, maybe four, times a week would be a good number.

"I think we should just go with it and see what happens," Brad responded. "After a year of daily sex, a little spontaneity might be nice." Well, he had a point. A little "fly by the seat of our pants" in the L-O-V-E department would be a *bit* of a change. Scheduling intimacy every day for the last 365 days put it at the top of the list, for sure, but made for few occasions for impulsiveness.

But I know the power of intention can be greater than the power of impulse (which is why exercising on impulse doesn't work for many of us, right?). So we've created a little intimacy hybrid. Brad rolls along on the spontaneity train and I'm secretly penciling in opportunities to ensure we stay on track. So far, it seems to be working–no tension, no awkwardness, no wondering when or if we're going to "do it" this week. Brad might initiate something after a great dinner out and I might turn to him during a commercial of *Project Runway*. "Hey, we haven't had sex since Monday . . . wanna?" It's all good.

Third, we are happier. While I don't think it's possible to float on cloud nine every minute of every day (unless you're on a Vicodin and chardonnay cocktail or something), we are a happier, more connected couple. I would have told you our marriage was in a good place before, but this kind of giant shared experience can't help but be transforming. It's like scaling a mountain you've never scaled before. I simply had no idea how beautiful the vistas would be. I'm more open to intimacy and Brad is less gaming for it because we have a better understanding of each other's needs and priorities. And when you team up on that kind of project, it's not so hard to team up on doing the dishes, managing the kids, and getting the cat fixed.

And finally, what in the heck possessed me to write a book about this?

Yes, well, I certainly did not set out to write a book about daily intimacy with my husband. I'm a middle-aged, part-time working mom of two living in the 'burbs. There is nothing remotely special about me (surely you know that by now) except for the fact that I can throw a mean dinner party and that I tried to have sex every day for a year with my good-natured husband, who was quite happy to oblige. I've never written a book before, I'm not a professional journalist or an English major (all you English majors out there, please be gentle with me).

I've published some essays locally, but they were in the Junior League magazine, for crying out loud, which means I wrote them for free. And while I've discovered in this process that nearly half of America aspires to write a book, never in a million years did I think I would write one about intimacy. I mean, come on! Neither, of course, did my parents. In fact, when I (finally) shared the news with them, my mom exclaimed with delight, "I just knew one day you would write a children's book!" Not exactly, Mom, but thanks for the vote of confidence. And my dad? Well, he's still working through it.

But over the course of the year I was so amazed at how this experiment resonated with women I've spoken with that I thought it would be good to share my experience. It seems that we all share the same frustrations, challenges, and issues regarding sex and intimacy with our spouses. Jean Anouilh said this: "To say yes, you have to sweat and roll up your sleeves and plunge both hands into life up to the elbows. It is easy to say no, even if saying no means death."

Well, after all is said and done, that's what I did. I said yes to my husband for a year and plunged both hands into my marriage up to my elbows.

Charla Muller
July 2008